One-to-One Training

One-to-One Training

Instructional Procedures for Learners with Developmental Disabilities

◆◆◆◆◆◆◆◆◆◆◆◆◆◆◆◆◆◆◆◆◆

Pieter C. Duker,
Robert Didden,
and
Jeff Sigafoos

pro·ed
An International Publisher

8700 Shoal Creek Boulevard
Austin, Texas 78757-6897
800/897-3202 Fax 800/397-7633
www.proedinc.com

© 2004 by PRO-ED, Inc.
8700 Shoal Creek Boulevard
Austin, Texas 78757-6897
800/897-3202   Fax 800/397-7633
www.proedinc.com

Library of Congress Cataloging-in-Publication Data

Duker, Pieter C., 1946–
    One-to-one training : instructional procedures for learners with developmental
    disabilities / Pieter Duker, Robert Didden, and Jeff Sigafoos.
        p. cm.
    Includes bibliographical references and index.
    ISBN 0-89079-980-6
    1. Developmentally disabled children—Education.   2. Individualized instruction.
I. Didden, Robert.   II. Sigafoos, Jeff.   III. Title.

LC4019.D85   2004
371.94—dc22   2003060299

This book is designed in Janson Text and Futura.

Printed in the United States of America

1   2   3   4   5   6   7   8   9   10   07   06   05   04   03

Contents

◆◆◆◆◆◆◆◆◆◆◆◆◆◆◆◆◆◆◆◆◆◆◆◆◆◆◆◆◆◆◆◆◆◆

Chapter 3

Multiple-Component Response Training ◆ *69*

Chapter 4

Preference Assessment and Choice Making ◆ *87*

Chapter 5

Managing Problem Behavior During Training ◆ *117*

Chapter 6
Maintenance and Generalization ◆ 145

Preface

◆◆◆◆◆◆◆◆◆◆◆◆◆◆◆◆◆◆◆◆◆◆◆◆◆◆◆◆

The severity—and hence the impact on learning—of a developmental disability is a joint function of the cause or etiology of the condition, the degree of intellectual impairment, the extent of adaptive behavior development, and the frequency and severity of problem behavior, if any. The contribution of etiology, intellectual impairment, adaptive functioning, and problem behavior to learning no doubt varies from individual to individual. Because the trainer can do nothing about etiology, his or her task becomes how best to improve adaptive behavior functioning and reduce problem behaviors so as to lessen the severity of the individual's disability on daily functioning. Teaching adaptive behaviors and reducing problem behaviors are the main instructional objectives of an educational program. In this book we focus on how to teach adaptive skills to individuals with developmental disabilities. We also focus on how to manage problem behaviors that may occur during adaptive skill training.

This book focuses exclusively on establishing adaptive behaviors through a one-to-one training format. One-to-one training is a structured approach that involves creating an opportunity for the learner to make the response, ensuring that a correct response is obtained from the learner, and then providing reinforcement for correct responses. This structured approach to training is also referred to as discrete-trial training. This focus excludes information on teaching in groups, which is generally less effective when initially attempting to teach new adaptive behaviors to individuals with severe to profound developmental disabilities.

The one-to-one teaching format implies the involvement of a learner (i.e., the individual with developmental disability) and a trainer. The level of adaptive behavior that can be attained by the learner through training depends to a large extent on the trainer's experience and skills. A degree in psychology, education, or even special education is no guarantee that the trainer will be effective in establishing an appropriate environment that will enable learners with developmental disabilities to acquire the skills targeted for instruction. Those hoping to become effective trainers need not only more explicit guidance for undertaking training, such as is presented in this book, but also the opportunity to practice the procedures described in this book. They need to understand the procedures, as well as gain practice and experience in using the procedures while being supervised by an experienced clinician.

In the 1960s and early 1970s, psychologists began investigating the use of behavioral principles to teach adaptive behavior skills to individuals with developmental disabilities. Skills such as following instructions, motor and verbal imitation, and attending to materials, as well as communication, motor, self-care, recreation and leisure, and social interaction skills, became targets of training. Limitations in the conventional behavioral techniques of reinforcing correct responses and correcting or ignoring incorrect responses soon became apparent. Although the general behavioral principles underlying educational approaches for individuals with developmental disabilities are still relevant, this book reflects the advances made in instructional procedures since these initial early efforts.

The nature of the skill that the trainer is trying to teach will determine whether a single-component or a multiple-component response training strategy should be used. Examples of single-component training include teaching a learner to respond to verbal instructions, produce manual signs, or point to the picture that matches an object. Multiple-component responses consist of a series of single-component responses, also called response chains. Examples of multiple-component training include teaching a learner to cook an egg, change a flat tire on a bicycle, pay for items in a grocery store, and use the toilet independently.

Before initiating any training program, the trainer needs to determine which objects or activities can be used to reinforce the learner's correct responses during training. Problem behavior may occur during training. The trainer needs to manage these behaviors during training so they do not continue to interfere with training. Once the new skill is taught, issues of maintenance and generalization need to be considered to ensure that the skills continue to be used appropriately after training. This book outlines procedures for accomplishing these goals during one-to-one training involving learners with developmental disabilities.

Chapter 1

◆◆◆◆◆◆◆◆◆◆◆◆◆◆◆◆◆◆◆◆◆◆◆◆◆◆◆◆◆◆◆

Single-Component Response Training: Prompting Sequences

Chapters 1 and 2 describe procedures for teaching new responses to learners with developmental disabilities. The procedures are intended for use in a one-to-one instructional format with one trainer and one learner. One-to-one instruction is often necessary to promote the learner's acquisition of new responses. Training begins by teaching a single-component response and then introducing other and more complicated multiple-component responses, but only as the learner makes progress and the trainer gains greater confidence in his or her teaching abilities.

A *single-component response* is a single, discrete response. Examples of single-component responses include pressing a switch to operate a cassette tape recorder, producing the manual sign "Eat" to request a preferred snack food, naming an object by pointing to the matching photograph, and pouring water into a cup. In contrast, a *multiple-component response* involves more than one response. Examples of multiple-component responses include dressing, preparing a meal, brushing one's teeth, going to the toilet, playing a video game, feeding a pet, shopping for groceries, and clearing the dinner dishes from the table. Chapters 1 and 2 outline instructional procedures for teaching single-component responses. Chapter 3 explains how these procedures are used to teach multiple-component responses.

Various instructional procedures can be used for single-component response training: most-to-least prompting, least-to-most prompting, time delay, graduated guidance, response delay, stimulus prompting, response shaping, behavior chain interruption, cues–pause–point training, response restriction, and imitation. Each procedure can be effective for teaching new skills to learners with developmental disabilities and for transferring the stimulus control of these skills so as to ensure more independent performance. Transfer of stimulus control is, therefore, a crucial concept in instructional technology. Transfer of stimulus control refers to a range of procedures that are designed to eliminate the need for prompts so that more appropriate or natural stimuli, not the trainer's prompts, come to control the response. In this chapter we consider the various ways that trainers can arrange prompting sequences to ensure that the learner acquires the single-component responses targeted for instruction. We discuss most-to-least prompting, least-to-most prompting, and combining the two procedures. We also provide information on withdrawing response prompts. In Chapter 2 we cover the additional single-component response training procedures mentioned in the previous paragraph. These additional procedures deal more extensively with transfer of stimulus control.

MOST-TO-LEAST PROMPTING

In a most-to-least, or decreasing assistance, procedure, prompts are arranged hierarchically from the most intrusive to the least intrusive. The first prompt provided is the one that already reliably evokes the desired response from the learner. Over successive opportunities or trials, this prompt is faded and replaced by less intrusive prompts. A typical most-to-least prompting hierarchy begins with providing hand-over-hand physical guidance to move the learner through the motions of the response. Along with physical guidance, the trainer should model the desired response, point to the object involved, and give an appropriate verbal instruction. For example, a trainer might use hand-over-hand guidance to physically assist a child to grasp a cup. This physical guidance is used to ensure that the desired response of holding the cup occurs during the training session.

Another example is when a trainer gently lifts a learner to prompt the response of getting up from a chair. After a number of such prompts, the amount of physical guidance is gradually reduced or faded; that is, the trainer provides less and less physical guidance while continuing to give the less intrusive prompts, such as modeling the correct response, providing a gesture prompt (i.e., pointing), or giving verbal instructions. At some point the learner should no longer need physical guidance, which becomes evident when the learner starts to make the correct response to the other, less intrusive prompts. At this point stimulus control has been transferred from the physical prompt to another, less intrusive prompt (see Chapter 2 for more details on transfer of stimulus control procedures). After this, the trainer withdraws the model prompt across a number of trials by gradually fading it out—that is, by modeling less and less of the desired behavior.

As the modeling is faded, the learner's response should come to be controlled by the gesture (i.e., pointing) and verbal prompts. As the gesture prompt is faded by making the pointing gesture less and less directed and holding the point for less and less time, the learner's response should come under the control of the verbal prompt alone. The latter is then considered to be the least intrusive prompt.

Prompts representing different levels of intrusiveness should be presented simultaneously, or as simultaneously as possible, at each trial, rather than successively. After several simultaneous presentations involving all of the prompts, the more intrusive prompt is faded, and control by the less intrusive prompt(s) is maintained.

Consider the following example. The learner and trainer are seated at a table. On the table in front of the learner are two objects: a coffee cup and a water glass. The trainer is teaching the learner the skill of discriminating between the two objects, which is technically a receptive labeling task. This skill is being taught because it is relevant to a restaurant work setting where the learner must be able to bring customers a coffee cup or a water glass, depending on what they want to drink. To teach the discrimination, the trainer provides 20 opportunities for the learner to respond during each instructional session. Instructional sessions are conducted once or twice per day, and 30 to 40 sessions may be required to teach the skill. Each opportunity begins with the trainer asking, "Which one do you use for coffee?" or "Which one do you use for water?" After giving the cue, the trainer initially uses the most intrusive prompt (physical assistance) by providing complete hand-over-hand guidance. Specifically, the trainer picks up the learner's hand and moves it so that the learner's hand touches the correct object. At the same time, the trainer gives a verbal prompt (i.e., either "touch cup" or "touch glass") and a gesture prompt (i.e., pointing to the correct object). After each correct response, the trainer provides less and less physical assistance, until it is no longer necessary to use any physical assistance.

After stopping physical assistance, the trainer begins fading out the gesture prompt by pointing less directly to the correct object and by pointing for less time. When the learner is correct at this level, the gesture prompt is faded completely. The final stage of intervention involves fading out the verbal prompt. The trainer fades the verbal prompt ("touch cup" and "touch glass") by saying only "cup" or "glass" and by saying the words more softly and then omitting the verbal prompt altogether. Through this procedure, the learner will learn to independently select the cup when the trainer asks, "Which one is used for coffee?" and to select the glass when the trainer asks, "Which one is used for water?"

The most-to-least-intrusive prompt hierarchy is highly effective and has been used to teach a variety of skills to learners with developmental disabilities. Because the trainer begins with the prompt that reliably results in the occurrence of the response (i.e., complete hand-over-hand physical guidance), the amount of time between the prompt and the learner's response is minimal. With this procedure, the learner moves through the task relatively quickly and receives immediate reinforcement, which is critical for promoting rapid acquisition of new skills (see Chapter 4). In addition, training time is reduced and used more efficiently. Furthermore, opportunities for errors are minimized because the first prompt given is the one that typically results in the correct response. In fact, most-to-least prompting procedures are sometimes referred to as an application of errorless learning procedures, because initially learners have less opportunity to make errors. Technically, most-to-least prompting should be viewed as one way of decreasing the probability of errors because it might still be possible for the learner to make an error when using a most-to-least prompt hierarchy.

For these reasons, most-to-least prompting may result in rapid skill acquisition with few errors.

On the other hand, the procedure has some drawbacks. Foremost among these is that it is often difficult for the trainer to determine precisely when a prompt should be withdrawn or faded. For example, when physical guidance is used as the most intrusive prompt, the decision about when to move to a less intrusive level of physical assistance or to some other prompt type (e.g., gesture prompt) depends on the trainer's ability to determine when the learner no longer requires physical guidance. Certain learner characteristics also might influence the effectiveness of a most-to-least hierarchy. If physical contact with the trainer is a reinforcer for the learner, then it may be difficult to fade this type of prompt. In contrast, other learners might actually dislike physical contact with a trainer, and this may lead some learners to resist physical guidance.

Although the trainer may have to use physical guidance during the early stages of training, in most cases it should be possible to move to less intrusive prompts relatively quickly because there are advantages for the learner to engage in the response more independently rather than having to be physically prompted. The advantages involve the fluency of response (i.e., it is often easier to do it oneself than to be physically guided through the motions) and more access to conditioned reinforcement (i.e., completing the task immediately precedes receipt of reinforcement and should therefore become a conditioned reinforcer). Complicating the trainer's job is the learner who is skilled at some but not all steps of a task. In this case, a trainer may need to combine various instructional procedures, such as using a most-to-least procedure for the more difficult steps of the task and a least-to-most procedure for the other steps.

The trainer also must consider the nature of the task that is to be trained. With some tasks (e.g., crossing a busy street), an incorrect response or error would be unacceptable. Because most-to-least prompting minimizes errors, it is the preferred strategy in such situations. A most-to-least hierarchy may also be indicated when teaching communication skills, such as manual signs or communicative gestures, particularly if the learner has a motor coordination problem or fails to imitate motor behaviors.

In addition to characteristics of the learner and task, the training environment itself might influence the trainer's decision to use a most-to-least prompt hierarchy. In some environments, it may be more efficient to use this procedure rather than, for example, a least-to-most prompt hierarchy. For instance, when a trainer is teaching a learner to request a cup of coffee in a café by pointing to a line drawing of a cup of coffee, it is perhaps more appropriate if the trainer initiates the sequence by physically guiding the learner to point to the symbol as opposed to verbally prompting, then gesturing, then pointing, before finally resorting to physical guidance.

Although most-to-least prompting has the advantage of providing more intensive instruction at an early point in time, a trainer must also be able to adapt it to the varying response demands of a task. Furthermore, the effectiveness of fixed prompt hierarchies over other procedures has not been empirically validated for all of the tasks that might be targeted for training. The preference of one hierarchy over another hierarchy, therefore, is based in part on trainer experience and preference, and perhaps other factors, rather than on the basis of empirical evidence alone.

LEAST-TO-MOST PROMPTING

With least-to-most prompting, also known as the increasing assistance model or system of least prompts, the trainer applies the least intrusive prompt first and then progresses through a sequence of increasingly intrusive prompts until the learner performs the target response. As the learner's performance improves across the training trials or sessions, the trainer reduces or fades the number and type of prompts until the learner responds to the natural cue(s) or least intrusive prompt only. In a typical least-to-most prompt hierarchy, the trainer first gives a verbal prompt or verbal instruction, then points to a referent object or picture, then models the response, and finally uses physical guidance. For example, in teaching a learner to request a preferred book by pointing to a corresponding line drawing on a communication board, the trainer might begin by offering the book (natural cue). If no response occurs, then the trainer would give a verbal prompt, "Point to the symbol." If the learner still fails to respond correctly, then the trainer would repeat the verbal prompt and also model the correct response of pointing to the symbol. If the learner again fails to respond correctly, then once again the trainer repeats the verbal prompt, models the response, and this time also physically guides the learner to point to the symbol. If possible, the trainer gives the prompts simultaneously. If this is not possible, the trainer should give prompts as close in time as possible and in their proper sequence (i.e., verbal, model, physical).

Once the learner begins to initiate the correct response, the trainer gradually withdraws the prompts by initially providing less and less physical guidance and then fading the model and verbal prompts. When the verbal prompt is successfully faded, the learner will be responding to the natural cue of the mere availability of the object. At this point, the learner's response is said to be more spontaneous (Halle, 1987).

As with most-to-least prompting, the least-to-most prompting procedure can be highly effective for teaching a range of communicative and other adaptive behaviors to individuals with developmental disabilities. Sigafoos, Doss, and Reichle (1989), for example, used least-to-most prompting to teach 3 adults with severe disabilities and no speech to request preferred objects. The response targeted for instruction was pointing to a line drawing corresponding to a needed object. To teach this type of graphic mode requesting, the learner was first given a preferred item (e.g., a cup of yogurt) but not the utensil that was needed to access that object (i.e., the spoon). After giving the preferred item, the trainer waited 10 seconds to allow the learner a chance to make the request. If the learner did not respond in 10 seconds, the trainer prompted the learner to point to the correct line drawing from a set of six drawings. Initially, a tact prompt was used if the learner did not make the correct request within 10 seconds. This involved holding up the needed item and asking "What is this?" If this did not evoke the correct response, then the next level of prompting was to model a correct response, and if necessary, the final level was to physically guide the learner's finger to point to the correct drawing. Prompts were faded by using a least-to-most hierarchy and providing less and less physical guidance. This procedure was effective in teaching all of the learners to request each of three needed items.

Least-to-most prompting is one of the most frequently used training procedures. Because the prompting sequence always begins with the least intrusive prompt and progresses to more intrusive prompts, it is a relatively easy procedure to use. The criterion for moving from one prompt to the next is easy to understand: If the learner does not respond correctly, then the trainer moves to the next level of prompt in the hierarchy.

If the learner responds correctly, then the trainer provides reinforcement and moves on to the next step of the task or the next trial in the training session.

In contrast to the most-to-least procedure, the least-to-most prompting procedure allows more opportunities for errors. With least-to-most prompting, the trainer provides the least intrusive prompt and then waits a predetermined length of time (e.g., 3 or 5 or 10 seconds) before proceeding to the next prompt level. Waiting allows the learner the opportunity to respond but also creates an opportunity for the learner to make an error. Some learners may make an error, which then needs to be corrected. Other learners, however, may simply wait for a more intrusive prompt because this may require less effort on their part. Fading physical guidance, usually the most intrusive prompt in the hierarchy, may also prove difficult if the learner becomes prompt dependent or is reinforced by physical contact with the trainer.

As with most-to-least prompting, characteristics of the task may affect the decision to use least-to-most prompting. For example, when a line of customers is waiting behind the learner in a shop, using a least-to-most prompting procedure to teach the person to purchase items may be contraindicated because it would take too long and hence be inconsiderate to other customers. On the other hand, if the response is already in the learner's repertoire and there is no real hurry to complete the task, such as when teaching a learner to engage in a leisure activity, then least-to-most prompting might be preferred over most-to-least prompting.

A number of useful variations of the least-to-most prompting procedure have been reported in the training literature. Horner and Keilitz (1975), for example, taught adolescents with developmental disabilities to brush their teeth using a sequence of three prompt levels: (a) verbal instruction plus materials, (b) verbal instruction plus materials plus model, and (c) verbal instruction plus materials plus physical guidance. The trainers successively applied increasing levels of prompting if the learner did not respond to less intrusive amounts of assistance. In another study, Giangreco (1983) employed a least-to-most prompting sequence of verbal instruction, gesture, model, and physical guidance to teach photography skills to a learner with developmental disabilities.

Wolery and Gast (1984) proposed four guidelines for using least-to-most prompting. First, the natural cue should be presented at each prompt level. Second, the trainer should deliver increasingly more information contingent upon an error or a nonresponse on the part of the learner. Third, a fixed wait time (often 5 or 10 seconds) should be inserted between each prompting level, thus allowing the learner time to respond independently. Fourth, trainers should deliver reinforcement for correct responses at all prompt levels. Consequently, a correct response at a given prompt level is reinforced. An incorrect response or nonresponse leads the trainer to implement more intrusive prompts until the learner makes the correct response, which is then reinforced. Reinforcement of all correct responses, even if these have to be physically prompted, may facilitate acquisition of the skill being taught. However, only those responses occurring in the presence of the natural cue alone (i.e., unprompted responses) count toward the criterion used to determine when the trainer should proceed to the next step of the task.

COMBINING MOST-TO-LEAST AND LEAST-TO-MOST PROMPTING

Sometimes a combination of most-to-least and least-to-most prompting procedures produces better outcomes than either procedure used alone. A combination of procedures can be useful for teaching communicative gestures or for teaching a range of responses that might be targeted in one-to-one training programs. Table 1.1 and the flowchart in Figure 1.1 give an overview of a combined procedure for teaching communicative gestures. As an aside, flowcharts originated from computer science and are helpful in clarifying complex procedures that involve many steps and decisions. In the language of flowcharts, a rectangle refers to an action, such as the presentation of a stimulus or reinforcement by the trainer. A diamond, in contrast, always

TABLE 1.1
Training Procedure for Communicative Gestures

Phase 1	Phase 2	Phase 3
• Present the model of the sign. • Point to the object/picture. • Say the name of the object/picture.	• Point to the object/picture. • Say the name of the object/picture.	• Say the name of the object/picture.
Give a reward for a correct response.	Give a reward for a correct response.	Give a reward for a correct response.
Move to Phase 2 of training when learner makes 3 consecutive correct responses.	Move to Phase 3 of training when learner makes 3 consecutive correct responses.	Move to training the next gesture beginning with Phase 1 when learner makes 3 consecutive correct responses.

Additional Supports

More Intrusive Prompt	*Modeling*	*Point to Object/Picture*
The amount of prompting is increased for each incorrect response or nonresponse. • ⅓ physical prompt • ⅔ physical prompt • ¾ physical prompt	The amount of prompting is increased for each incorrect response or nonresponse. • ⅓ model • ⅔ model • ¾ model	The amount of prompting is increased for each incorrect response or nonresponse. • ⅓ object • ⅔ object • ¾ object
When the learner responds correctly, begin withdrawing prompts. Then return to top of Phase 1.	When the learner responds correctly, begin withdrawing prompts. Then return to top of Phase 2.	When the learner responds correctly, begin withdrawing prompts. Then return to top of Phase 3.

Note. Adapted from *Teaching the Developmentally Handicapped Communicative Gesturing: A How-To-Do Book*, by P. Duker, 1988, Berwyn, PA: Swets North American. Copyright 1988 by Swets North American.

follows an action and always has two consequences: "no"—in which case one should return to the previous step or end the task—and "yes"—in which case one should go on with the training as indicated. In using a flowchart to guide the training

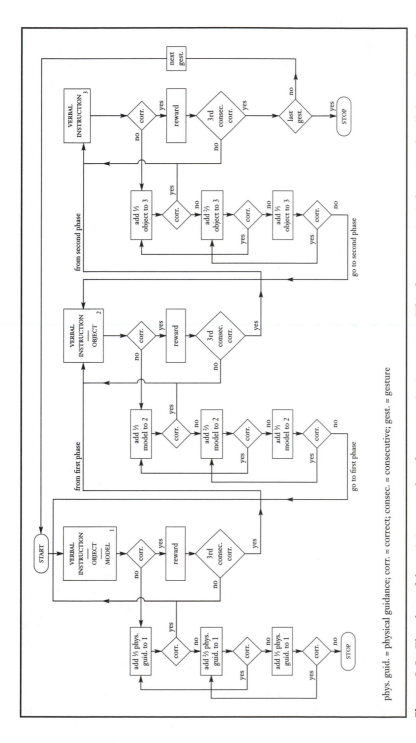

Figure 1.1. Flowchart of the training procedure for communicative gestures. This figure contains information for all three phases of training. Figures 1.2, 1.3, and 1.4 focus on Phases 1, 2, and 3, respectively. *Note.* From *Teaching the Developmentally Handicapped Communicative Gesturing: A How-To-Do Book,* by P. Duker, 1988, Berwyn, PA: Swets North American. Copyright 1988 by Swets North American. Reprinted with permission.

phys. guid. = physical guidance; corr. = correct; consec. = consecutive; gest. = gesture session, the trainer should follow the arrows, beginning with START and finishing with STOP. The flowchart should be read from left to right and from top to bottom. To become familiar with the parts of the flowchart, it may be worthwhile for the trainer to follow the track from START to STOP by putting a finger on the flowchart while trying to imagine what occurs at each point.

To illustrate the use of the flowchart, we begin with one communicative gesture along with the spoken instruction and its corresponding object or picture. The trainer demonstrates, or models, the gesture. This is referred to as the model of the gesture. After the learner's attention has been gained, as evidenced by making eye contact, the learner is asked to hold his or her hands in ready position, perhaps by placing hands in lap, and then the trainer

- presents the model of the sign,

- points to the object or picture at the same time or closely in time, and

- says the name of the object or picture.

This is an example of a most-to-least prompting hierarchy (i.e., model, gesture, verbal). For example, in teaching the manual sign for "I want a drink," the trainer models the gesture by touching his or her mouth with the closed fist and leaning his or her head slightly backward while pointing to a cup or glass containing a preferred beverage. The trainer also gives a clear verbal prompt, "Drink." Although a flowchart of the complete procedure is presented in Figure 1.1, the part that refers to this specific phase of training appears in Figure 1.2.

A verbal prompt involves saying the name of the object or picture, and the trainer uses this prompt throughout each phase of the training, whereas the trainer withdraws the other two more intrusive prompts in the second and third phases. The underlying assumption of the prompting hierarchy is that correctly responding to a verbal instruction is more difficult for the learner than responding to the trainer's model of the gesture. However, this may not always be a valid assumption. There are large differences between learners in this respect. For example,

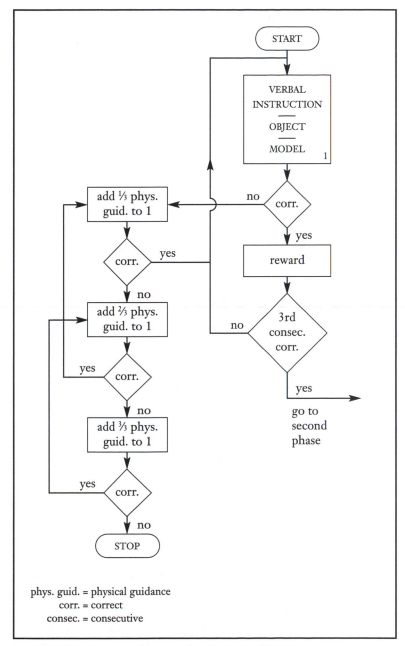

Figure 1.2. Flowchart for Phase 1 of training. *Note.* From *Teaching the Developmentally Handicapped Communicative Gesturing: A How-To-Do Book,* by P. Duker, 1988, Berwyn, PA: Swets North American. Copyright 1988 by Swets North American. Reprinted with permission.

in our experience, learners with severe autism tend not to respond to modeling of a manual sign and often need prolonged physical guidance to learn to make a communicative gesture. On the other hand, learners with developmental disabilities who are also deaf and children with Down syndrome are often much more responsive to modeled prompts than are children with autism.

Technically, the training procedure outlined in the table and the flowchart combines most-to-least prompting and least-to-most prompting. The learner is exposed to an initial phase in which more intrusive prompts are used, but then moves to a training phase in which less intrusive prompts are provided. Least-to-most prompting in this procedure involves a gradual increase in the level or intrusiveness of prompting following an incorrect response. If the learner makes a correct response, however, the trainer immediately gives the reinforcer. Reinforcement should be given only if the response is performed correctly and completely in line with the defined requirements. Reinforcement of sloppy, ill-formed, incomplete, or poorly articulated responses is harmful because it teaches the individual to make the response incorrectly. When teaching manual signs, such reinforcement may result in signs that are too ambiguous. It is better to prompt a response to make sure it is performed well than to reinforce poor examples of the response. It is also advisable to have a third person occasionally monitor the training session to judge whether the produced gestures meet the defined requirements. The trainer may be unaware that his or her criteria have changed unintentionally over time.

If the learner begins to produce a movement that will undoubtedly result in an incorrect response, the trainer should quickly interrupt this movement to prevent the error (Duker, 1981). The trainer should not allow the learner to complete the incorrect response. Contrary to what some educators and trainers believe, giving learners with developmental disabilities the opportunity to make errors does not give them any information that may help them to avoid such errors in the future. On the contrary, if errors are allowed to occur, they are more likely to persist. In addition, making an error may cause the learner to experience negative emotional responses, which actually interfere with the training sessions and the learning process.

Consider again Phase 1 of training, shown in Figure 1.2. If the learner fails to make the correct response or makes no response—which is in fact very likely during the initial teaching sessions—then the trainer must repeat the appropriate instruction and simultaneously apply the more intrusive physical prompt. This is shown on the left side of Figure 1.2. This physical guidance might consist of taking gentle hold of the learner's hands, forming them into the correct shape, and then moving the hands so as to make the response. An important consideration is when the trainer should introduce this prompt. As a general rule, we suggest that the trainer move on to the more intrusive prompt if the learner has not begun to initiate the response within 10 seconds.

Another issue that the trainer must consider is the amount of physical guidance to provide. Generally, the idea is to give the least amount of physical guidance that is necessary to prompt the correct response. The degree of physical guidance might be viewed along a continuum that has three markers. If complete hand-over-hand guidance is considered the greatest amount of prompt, the flowchart shows that initially one third of this amount of physical guidance is used (as indicated by the directive to "add ⅓ phys. guid." in the flowchart). This amount translates into tapping the elbow or lightly touching and slightly moving the learner's arm. If this amount of physical guidance is not enough to prompt the correct response, then the trainer should use a two-thirds level of physical guidance, which equates to moving the learner's arm into the appropriate position. If this still is not enough, then the trainer actually molds the learner's hand(s) and arm(s) into the correct position and guides them through the motion necessary to make the response.

During the process of increasing (from one third to two thirds to three thirds) or decreasing (from three thirds to two thirds to one third) physical guidance, a correct response should occur at some point. When the learner makes a correct response, the trainer reduces the amount of physical guidance on the next trial. If no response occurs, then the next more intrusive level of physical prompt is used. If the learner begins to make an error, then the trainer interrupts the response and gives a more intrusive level of physical prompt.

In Phase 1 of training, the learner at some point will acquire the first response (e.g., the manual sign for "drink"), and it is then appropriate to begin teaching a second response (e.g., the manual sign for "puzzle"). This part of the training begins by presenting only the verbal instruction as a prompt for the second response. While giving the verbal instruction—and this is very important—the trainer should prevent the learner from making a response to that instruction, because the learner would most likely make an error by producing the first response, instead of the second. The learner, therefore, must be taught not to respond initially to the verbal prompt for the second gesture so as to prevent the inevitable error. Although this requirement of initially preventing the second response may seem counterintuitive, it will in fact speed the acquisition of the second response in the long run. Such a procedure is called *inhibition training*.

During inhibition training, the extent to which the learner is prevented from responding to the verbal instruction is then gradually decreased until the learner independently withholds the response. Through this procedure the learner is taught to discriminate between the one instruction he or she should respond to (i.e., the verbal prompt for the first response) and the other instruction that he or she should not yet respond to (i.e., the verbal prompt for the second response).

Inspection of Figure 1.1 shows that Phase 1 of training is complete when the learner makes three consecutive correct responses. At this point Phase 2 of training begins, which involves use of verbal instruction and the object prompt, but not use of the model. The point of Phase 2 is to retain correct responding while the model prompt is eliminated. Again, before giving the verbal instruction, the trainer must gain the learner's attention, make eye contact, and get the learner's hands into the ready position (e.g., hands on lap). After this the trainer points to the object or picture and says its name (e.g., "Drink"). In Phase 1 the trainer also models the response, but modeling is not done in Phase 2. As always, a correct response is immediately reinforced and errors are interrupted.

Consider, for example, that the learner is being taught to make the manual sign for *bicycle* to request access to a bike for riding during playtime. The manual sign consists of making a fist with each hand and rotating the fists alternately in front of one's own chest, as if simulating the pedaling motion that one makes while riding a bike. If the learner fails to make the correct response or does not respond within about 10 seconds, the trainer models the correct response by demonstrating the sign to the learner. The trainer also simultaneously points to the picture or the bicycle and gives the verbal instruction, "Bicycle." The prompting sequence involving the model would begin by giving only one third of the model. For example, the trainer might place both fists in front of his or her own chest for only 1 to 2 seconds. This should remind the learner to respond with the correct gesture. This level of modeling is indicated by "add ⅓ model" in the flowchart of Figure 1.3.

If the learner still does not begin to make the correct response, additional prompting is needed. The trainer, therefore, increases the amount of the modeling prompt. For example, the trainer places his or her own fists at chest level and begins to rotate them (two-thirds model). If the learner still does not make the correct sign, then the trainer moves on to presenting the complete (three-thirds) model, which involves rotating the fists repeatedly as if pedaling a bicycle. If, however, the learner gives a correct response at this level, the trainer reduces the amount of the model given by presenting the two-thirds model in the next trial and so forth.

After the learner makes three consecutive correct responses to the presentation of the object or picture plus verbal instruction, the trainer proceeds to Phase 3 of the training, in which the object or picture prompt is withdrawn as well. Phase 3 of training is shown in Figure 1.4. *Phase 3 of training is not appropriate for learners with hearing impairment or those who fail to process auditory information.*

The third phase of training starts, as always, with first getting the learner's attention and making sure the learner is ready for the trial. The trainer says the name of the object or picture (e.g., "Drink" or "Bicycle"). At this phase, however, only the verbal instruction is used; the object or picture is not present. As before, correct responses are immediately reinforced; that is, the learner signs "drink" and receives a preferred drink or signs "bicycle" and is allowed to ride the bike. The trainer interrupts incorrect responses as quickly as possible.

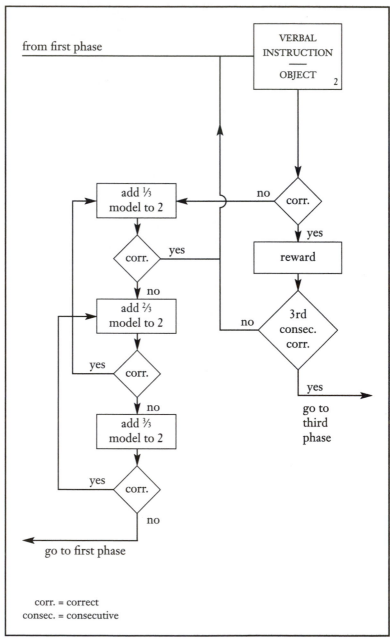

Figure 1.3. Flowchart for Phase 2 of training. *Note.* From *Teaching the Developmentally Handicapped Communicative Gesturing: A How-To-Do Book,* by P. Duker, 1988, Berwyn, PA: Swets North American. Copyright 1988 by Swets North American. Reprinted with permission.

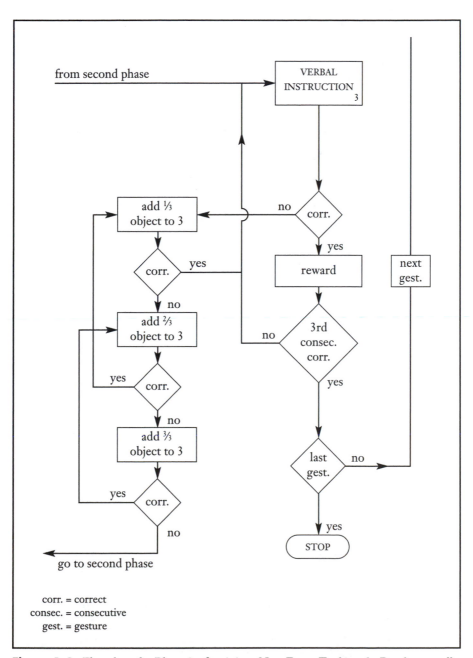

Figure 1.4. Flowchart for Phase 3 of training. *Note.* From *Teaching the Developmentally Handicapped Communicative Gesturing: A How-To-Do Book,* by P. Duker, 1988, Berwyn, PA: Swets North American. Copyright 1988 by Swets North American. Reprinted with permission.

If the learner fails to respond correctly or does not respond to the verbal instruction only, the trainer must reintroduce the object or picture to prompt a correct response. On the next trial, the trainer points to the object or picture while saying its name. This is called *one-third object* and is indicated by "add ⅓ object" in the flowchart of Figure 1.4. If the learner makes an incorrect response or no response within 10 seconds after presentation of the instruction, the trainer should use increasing levels of prompts. At the next level, the trainer touches the object or picture for 1 second (*two-thirds object*). If the learner still fails to make a correct response, the trainer holds the object or picture (*three-thirds object*) in the next trial. If a correct response occurs during the process of fading, the trainer begins to withdraw assistance by moving from three thirds to two thirds to one third. This approach has proven to be highly effective (Duker, 1988; Duker & Michielsen, 1983; Duker & Morsink, 1984; Duker & van Lent, 1991).

WITHDRAWING RESPONSE PROMPTS

The psychologist B. F. Skinner (1968) considered the notion of withdrawal of prompts during the learning process. He argued that if a learner is to emit the target response reliably without the assistance of prompts, then that response must come under the control of the natural or discriminative stimuli for that response (i.e., stimuli that are naturally present when it is appropriate to make that response). However, if the prompt continues to exercise control over the response, the natural stimuli will fail to gain control over this response. Therefore, the trainer must consider how to reduce or fade the degree of control exercised by the prompt. This cannot be achieved by sudden withdrawal of the initial prompt, because the natural stimuli have not yet acquired any reliable control over the response. Rather, this is achieved by a gradual reduction in the control of the prompt so as to build up the degree of control exercised by the natural stimuli.

Therefore, the trainer must ensure that the training process does not end before prompts have been successfully withdrawn or faded. If the skills are to be functional for the learner, then the trainer needs to make sure that the newly acquired responses occur reliably in the presence of the natural cues without having to be prompted by the trainer. In teaching manual signs, for example, the learner needs to make the correct sign without the trainer having to point to the object, model the sign, or physically prompt the learner to make the sign. The responses must be taught in such a way that they come under control of natural or discriminative stimuli for that response (i.e., stimuli that are naturally present when it is appropriate to make that response). If the instructional prompts used in training continue to exercise control over the response, then the natural discriminative stimuli will fail to gain control over this response.

As mentioned before, the trainer should not suddenly withdraw the instructional prompt unless the natural stimuli have acquired reliable control over the response. Instead, the trainer should implement procedures that lead to a gradual reduction of the control exerted by instructional prompts, while simultaneously bringing the response under the control of the accompanying natural discriminative stimuli until the natural cues control the response without the need for any instructional prompts.

Withdrawing prompts is a difficult process (see, e.g., Touchette & Howard, 1984). Doing it well requires the trainer to make several decisions. If the prompts are withdrawn too quickly, errors may occur. If they are withdrawn too slowly, they may become difficult to fade completely because the learner may become dependent in the sense of always needing some level of prompting. Decisions about prompt withdrawal are, therefore, crucial to the long-term success of any training program.

We recommend using a three-step process for fading prompts, as outlined in Figures 1.1 through 1.4. Whether the trainer is using physical guidance (Figure 1.2), modeling (Figure 1.3), or a gesture prompt consisting of pointing to the object (Figure 1.4), the process starts with providing only one third of the prompt. If the one-third prompt is not effective, then the trainer increases the intrusiveness of the prompt to the two-thirds level. If this is still not effective, then the trainer advances to giving the complete (three-thirds) prompt.

Despite the importance of withdrawal of response prompts, few guidelines exist, and those that do are often poorly defined and lack empirical support. In discussing the guidelines provided in the literature, we first consider those of a more general nature and then those of a more specific nature. The general guidelines can be assigned to two categories. The first, consistent with the most-to-least prompt hierarchy, suggests that each successive prompt in the hierarchy should offer less assistance. The second general guideline suggests that the trainer should progressively reduce the intrusiveness of the prompts. For example, physical guidance is assumed be more intrusive than a verbal instruction. A move from a physical prompt to a verbal instruction, therefore, may represent a reduction in intrusiveness. However, certain physical prompts (e.g., moving the learner's hand to the vicinity of a cup that has to be grasped) may provide less assistance to a verbally competent learner than a related verbal instruction (e.g., "Pick up the cup"). Moving from a complete to a partial verbal instruction (e.g., from "Pick up the cup" to "Cup") reduces the degree of assistance provided, but it does not necessarily reduce the intrusiveness of the prompt.

According to specific guidelines, two classes of prompt hierarchy can be distinguished: those that use prompts from different modalities (i.e., physical, visual, or verbal) and those that use prompts from the same modality (i.e., partial model, complete model, or repeated complete model). More common is the use of prompts from different modalities, such as a most-to-least hierarchy involving physical, model, gesture, and finally verbal prompts; however, this hierarchy is not entirely consistent with the two general guidelines discussed above. Thus, a move from physical to model to gesture to verbal prompts does not necessarily involve a move from more to less assistance. For example, a partial physical prompt (e.g., one-third physical guidance) may provide much less assistance to a verbally competent learner than a complete verbal instruction, and pointing to the part of the materials that must be manipulated (i.e., a gesture prompt) may provide less assistance than a verbal instruction, as the gesture may indicate only what to manipulate, not how to manipulate it.

The current conceptualization of prompt hierarchies is also often inconsistent with the notion that fading should reduce the intrusiveness of the prompts. For example, verbal prompts are not always less noticeable and hence less intrusive than gesture or visual prompts or even physical guidance. Also, use of the three modalities is not appropriate in all circumstances or with all learners. For example, verbal instructions may not be effective for those who have problems in processing speech or who function in a noisy environment.

Wilcox and Bellamy (1982) proposed a novel type of prompt hierarchy in which all prompts belong to the same modality. Such hierarchies, they suggested, would permit the trainer to focus on a mode of prompt best suited to the learner, task, and setting, and yet maintain the ability of trainers to provide more or less prompting as needed in relation to the learner's performance.

Along these same lines, Lovaas, Koegel, and Schreibman (1979) distinguished between within-stimulus prompts and extra-stimulus prompts. Within-stimulus prompts are prompts from the same modality as the stimulus that controls the response. For example, a spoon might be shown to a learner to prompt her to use the right utensil at mealtime. An extra-stimulus prompt, in contrast, refers to a prompt that is from a different modality from the natural cue. To prompt spoon use, the trainer might say, "Use the spoon" or show a picture of the spoon. Some learners with autism actually seem to learn better when within-stimulus prompts are used, but these prompts may limit the range of responses that can be taught because it may be hard to find an effective prompt that matches the modality of the natural cue.

Schreibman (1975) described a fading process involving within-stimulus prompts for teaching visual discrimination skills. The process is illustrated in Figure 1.5. With Step 5 as the target stimulus, training begins with Step 1 and moves through the steps while errors are kept to a minimum. Specifically, the goal is to teach the learner to point to the S^+ and not to the S^-. Figure 1.5 shows a process for teaching this skill using within-stimulus prompting. In the top series (1), the S^- is gradually faded into the task. For example, the left sequence

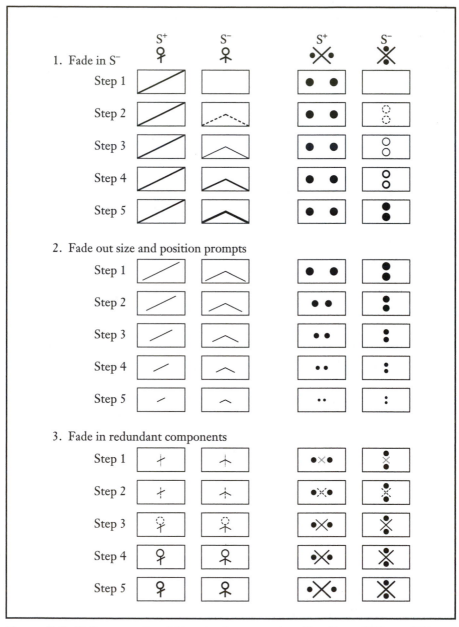

Figure 1.5. Fading steps for within-stimulus prompting. *Note.* From "Effects of Stimulus and Extrastimulus Prompting on Discrimination Learning in Autistic Children," by L. Schreibman, 1975, *Journal of Applied Behavior Analysis, 8,* pp. 91–112. Copyright 1975 by The Society for the Experimental Analysis of Behavior, Inc. Reprinted with permission.

in Step 1 indicates that the learner sees two rectangular cards. One card (the S⁺) has a diagonal line through it, and the other card (the S⁻) is blank. The correct response requires the learner to point to the S⁺ and not to the S⁻. As you can see from Figure 1.5, lines are gradually added to the blank card in Steps 2 through 5, thereby making the discrimination between the S⁺ and the S⁻ more difficult. Although the discrimination becomes more difficult at each step, the correct response remains the same in that the learner should point to the S⁺ and not to the S⁻. A similar progression from an easy to a more difficult discrimination between cards with dots on them is shown in the right sequence of the top series. In the middle series (2), the S⁺ and S⁻ are gradually made smaller, thereby making them less easy to discriminate. For example, consider the right sequence shown in the middle series (2). In Step 1, the learner sees two cards. Both cards have two dots. The difference is that with the S⁺ the two dots are arranged horizontally, whereas with the S⁻ the two dots are arranged vertically. Learners remain at Step 1 until they are consistently correct in pointing to the S⁺ and rarely or never point to the S⁻. Such consistency shows that they are making the discrimination based on horizontal versus vertical arrangement of dots. Next, in Steps 2 through 5 the dots on both cards become smaller and fainter, thereby making the discrimination more difficult.

In the bottom series (3), additional elements are added to the S⁺ and S⁻. For example, in the left sequence, the learner initially sees two cards. At Step 1, the S⁺ has a diagonal line and the S⁻ has the inverted v-shaped line. In addition, there are faint horizontal dots dividing each line. In Steps 2 through 5, these faint dots become more pronounced and a circle is added to the top of both the S⁺ and the S⁻, thereby making the discrimination more difficult.

The intention of Figure 1.5 is to illustrate within-stimulus prompting in which S⁺ and S⁻ stimuli are gradually altered from an initially easier discrimination (Step 1) to a more difficult discrimination (Step 5). Unlike the flowcharts presented earlier in this chapter, which involved a three-step fading process, Schreibman's process shown in Figure 1.5 involves a five-step process.

By contrast, as an example of a procedure of extra-stimulus prompting, the trainer might place the visual stimuli represented at Step 5 of Figure 1.5 in front of the learner and begin by pointing with his or her finger to the upper edge of the S^+ card on each trial. Pointing constitutes the extra-stimulus prompt. Then, the pointing prompt is gradually removed (e.g., from the top of the card to a position between the S^+ and S^- cards) while errors are kept to a minimum. Some evidence suggests that fewer training trials are needed and fewer errors are made if the trainer uses within-stimulus prompting as opposed to a procedure using extra-stimulus prompting (Schreibman, 1975), but in terms of developing the materials, it is often easier and more economical to use extra-stimulus prompts such as pointing and physical guidance than to construct a series of stimuli that incorporate within-stimulus prompting, such as those shown in Figure 1.5.

Another example in which extra-stimulus prompting may impair learning is the blocking effect of extra-stimulus prompts on sight-word reading. For learners with moderate developmental disabilities, sight words are usually taught using pictures of items represented by the sight words. However, presentation of the extra-stimulus prompt (i.e., a picture of the item represented by the word) may adversely affect the reading of sight words, a result that is attributed to a blocking effect by the extra-stimulus prompt. That is, previous learning of a verbal response (e.g., say "Ball") when shown a picture (i.e., photograph of a ball) may block the learning of the verbal response to its written equivalent (i.e., "B a l l") when the picture and the written word are presented simultaneously or as a compound stimulus. Didden, Prinsen, and Sigafoos (2000) showed that 6 learners with moderate disabilities learned sight words faster if the words were not presented together with the picture of the item than if they were presented together with the picture. The blocking effect of extra-stimulus prompts in the case of sight-word reading may be prevented from occurring when (written) sight words are presented without extra-stimulus prompts.

At another level of conceptualization, Billingsley and Romer (1983) distinguished between illustrative and symbolic prompts. Illustrative prompts provide a picture of the response and are, therefore, high in "iconicity," or resemblance to the response. An example would be the trainer's modeling of the manual sign that the learner is to make. Symbolic prompts, on the other hand, provide little or no iconicity. Examples include partial physical prompts, verbal instructions, and pointing. Symbolic prompts imply little assistance. However, whether or not symbolic prompts provide less assistance than illustrative prompts is questionable. For example, a complete verbal instruction (e.g., "Show me the sign for cup") to a verbally competent learner could provide as much assistance as modeling the manual sign.

Some help in deciding how to implement prompts comes from Riley (1993, 1995), who proposed guidelines for arranging the prompt hierarchy. The main guideline is that the prompt hierarchy should contain prompts that progressively decrease the amount of relevant information given to the learner. Transfer of stimulus control might be facilitated by replacing the initial prompt with one that provides less information. During the course of training, when moving from trial to trial, the trainer should move to using prompts that provide progressively less information as the learner responds to one level of prompt.

Some examples of how the informational content of prompts can be reduced, as suggested by Riley (1993, 1995), may be useful. For teaching a vocational skill such as attaching handles to cabinet doors, the trainer can model a response to provide information about what part of the task materials should be manipulated (hold handle to drilled holes in the cabinet, insert bolts, tighten bolts) and how the materials should be manipulated (tighten bolts by using screwdriver). The trainer can reduce the amount of information given by such a prompt by replacing it with a pointing prompt (e.g., pointing to screwdriver), which shows what should be manipulated but not how. The amount of information in a verbal prompt can be decreased by reducing the extent to which the instruction specifies the part of the task to be manipulated. For example, the informational content of "Tighten the bolts with the screwdriver" can be reduced to "Tighten with screwdriver" or simply "Screwdriver."

Riley (1993) conducted a number of studies that assessed the effectiveness of using faded prompts in accordance with the guidelines outlined above. The acquisition of both verbal knowledge and perceptual–motor skills was examined. In each study, an experimental condition in which the initial prompt continued to be used was compared to a condition in which the initial prompt was substituted by a faded prompt that was considered to provide less information. The learners in these studies were individuals with moderate to severe developmental disabilities. In one study, 2 learners were taught to prepare a snack. The continued presentation of a modeling prompt was compared with a condition in which the model was faded to a pointing prompt, on the assumption that pointing provided less information than modeling. The result was that transfer of stimulus control occurred more rapidly under the fading condition in which the model was replaced with the point.

In another study, Riley (1993) compared the same two conditions in teaching 3 learners to operate a cassette player. Again, training using the fading condition was more effective in terms of speed of learning, although the difference was small, possibly due to a ceiling effect. In a third study, 2 learners were taught the rules of a card game (specifically, how many cards to play in response to certain penalty cards). Continued presentation of a verbal instruction containing the rule was compared with a condition in which these instructions were faded to a question about the rule, which required the learner to choose between the correct number and an incorrect option. Both learners succeeded in following the rules in the fading condition but failed in the no-fading condition. Rules not learned in the latter condition were subsequently learned once fading was introduced. The data from Riley's studies suggest that trainers will be more effective in fading prompts when they consider the informational content provided by a prompt and seek to move from prompts that initially give much information to prompts that give progressively less information.

We now turn to the fading of physical guidance, an issue that requires special consideration. Physical guidance can be used to help the learner understand and recall task requirements, and in some situations it can be faded in accordance with the guideline of reducing the amount of information the prompt contains. Full physical guidance (the three thirds in Figure 1.2), which provides information about what to do and how to do it, can be faded to a partial physical prompt that provides information about what to manipulate (e.g., the learner's hand is moved to the vicinity of the object to be manipulated) but not how to manipulate the object (the two thirds and one third of Figure 1.2).

Physical guidance can also be used when the learner seems to understand and recall the task requirements but is unable to execute the task. Fading physical guidance in this situation is subject to somewhat different considerations. This situation may occur because the learner cannot exercise the necessary degree of motor precision or does not have the physical strength to perform the response, or cannot execute the different components of the task simultaneously. For example, a learner being taught to self-feed with a spoon may understand and recall the task requirements but does not have sufficient motor control to bring the spoon to his mouth. In such a situation, the learner may require practice to become fluent. In many cases, therefore, assisted practice using physical guidance may accelerate acquisition of the response—that is, the individual may learn to execute the response with greater speed and coordination when initially given repeated physical assistance to do so.

Physical guidance can be used to assist practice in this context. The rationale for fading guidance when used in this way is provided by the observation that the beneficial effects of practice are greater as the learner makes more of the response (i.e., exercises a greater degree of power and precision and performs a greater number of simultaneous components). Fading should involve gradually increasing the learner's involvement by gradually decreasing the control exercised by the trainer over the response, the number of simultaneous components performed by the trainer, or both.

SUMMARY AND CONCLUSION

Although one-to-one training, using the procedures described in this chapter, is highly effective for teaching single-component responses to learners with developmental disabilities, the effectiveness of the procedures depends to a large extent on the skills of the trainer. Becoming an effective trainer requires practice in using the procedures outlined in this chapter. It is also important to develop a training history in which the learner is successful. It is best for both trainer and learner to begin one-to-one training by targeting a single-component response. Keeping the initial teaching goal simple and focused on a single-component response will enable the trainer to concentrate on gaining fluency in using the procedures. Such a focus also increases the chances that the learner will experience success in acquiring the response. It is also important to make use of prompting procedures that will ensure that the response occurs and can be reinforced.

Ultimately, the goal of training is to ensure that the learner responds correctly without having to be prompted. Along these lines, this chapter includes a discussion of procedures that can be used to fade instructional prompts. The idea of fading is to transfer control of the response from instructional prompts to the natural cues in the environment that should set the occasion for the response. Because this transfer of stimulus control is so important, Chapter 2 describes additional transfer of stimulus control procedures, as well as presenting other procedures that are used in teaching single-component responses during one-to-one training.

Chapter 2

◆◆◆◆◆◆◆◆◆◆◆◆◆◆◆◆◆◆◆◆◆◆◆◆◆◆◆◆◆◆◆

Single-Component Response Training: Additional Procedures

This chapter builds on the material presented in Chapter 1 by considering additional transfer of stimulus control procedures. The trainer often needs to implement these types of procedures to fade the instructional prompts and ensure that the learner's response occurs in the presence of the relevant discriminative stimuli. To complement the procedures described in Chapter 1, this chapter covers the additional procedures of time delay, graduated guidance, response delay, stimulus prompting, response shaping, behavior chain interruption, cues–pause–point, response restriction, and imitation. Together these procedures and those described in Chapter 1 should enable the trainer to be effective in teaching new single-component responses to learners with developmental disabilities. Another issue considered in this chapter is stimulus overselectivity. Because stimulus overselectivity represents a problem of irrelevant stimulus control that has implications for the use of transfer of stimulus control procedures, it is discussed at the end of this chapter.

TIME DELAY

Time delay—also known as delayed cueing and delayed prompting—is one method for transferring stimulus control (Touchette, 1971). There are two types of time-delay procedures: progressive time delay and constant time delay.

With progressive time delay, the trainer waits increasing durations of time—for example, by increasing the duration of time from 1 second to 3 seconds to 5 seconds to 10 seconds, and so on—before prompting the learner for a response. This technique is used to transfer control from a stimulus that already controls the response to another stimulus that initially does not control the response. Because of this increasing duration, the term *progressive time delay* is used to differentiate the procedure from a similar procedure, *constant time delay*, in which the duration of delay is always the same (e.g., the trainer always waits 10 seconds before prompting).

Touchette's initial work on the time-delay procedure was published in 1971. In this study, he first taught 3 boys with developmental disabilities to press a key illuminated with a red light and not to press a simultaneously presented white lighted key. After the discrimination was established, black figures were superimposed on the lighted keys. The letter "E" with the legs pointing down was superimposed on the red key, and an "E" with the legs pointing up was superimposed on the white key. On the first trial, the black figures and lighted keys were presented simultaneously. A correct response in the first trial delayed the onset of the red stimulus by 0.5 second in the next trial. Thus, both figures occurred on white backgrounds for 0.5 second, then the red light was added to prompt the child to press the correct key. Thereafter, each correct response increased the delay in the presentation of the red light prompt by an additional 0.5 second and each error reduced the delay by 0.5 second.

Transfer of stimulus control was said to occur at the moment when the learner reliably responded to the correct black figure before the red light prompt appeared. With the use of this progressive time-delay procedure, all 3 boys transferred responding from the red key to the black figure. As it turned out, the moment of transfer tended to occur at around 3 seconds.

In an extended phase of the study, Touchette (1971) implemented a similar process in an attempt to transfer control from the red light to tilted lines. This time the progressive time-delay procedure was effective for 2 of the 3 boys; the third boy failed to learn the discrimination between the two sets of tilted lines even though the delay was extended to 17.5 seconds. In effect, this learner was correct only when the red light prompt was added, and hence he failed to obtain reinforcement for correct responses before the red light prompt. Perhaps this learner needed more trials with both stimuli presented simultaneously before the delay was introduced.

In a later study, Striefel, Bryan, and Aikins (1974) investigated the effectiveness of a modified version of the progressive time-delay procedure. Their goal was to teach 3 adolescents with developmental disabilities to respond to verbal instructions (e.g., "Push car"). Each learner had been taught to imitate all of the responses that were to be brought under the control of verbal instructions. The procedure used imitation, simultaneous, and delay trials. During imitation trials, the trainer said, "Do this," and modeled the response. If the learner responded correctly within 5 seconds, a reinforcer (i.e., preferred edible) was delivered immediately. An error or no response resulted in the trainer saying "No" and repeating the trial, except that immediately following modeling of the response, the trainer provided physical guidance and made a verbal statement ("Good!").

After three consecutive correct imitations of the response to be taught, simultaneous trials were initiated. During these trials the trainer gave the verbal instruction and modeled the response (i.e., a simultaneous trial). Correct responses were followed by reinforcement and errors by the correction procedure. After one correct response, delay trials were initiated in which a delay was inserted between the presentation of the verbal instruction and the modeling of the response. Each correct response resulted in a longer delay for the next trial. The delays increased from 0.5 second to 1 second and by 1-second increments thereafter. Errors resulted in using the correction procedure and reducing the delay by reverting to the previous delay interval.

This procedure can result in at least five types of responses:

1. *Correct anticipations*—The learner responds correctly before the prompt is given (i.e., before the modeling prompt).

2. *Correct responses* or *correct waits*—The learner responds correctly following the prompt given by the trainer.

3. *Nonwait errors*—The learner responds incorrectly before the prompt is given.

4. *Incorrect waits*—The learner makes an error after the prompt is given.

5. *No response*—The learner fails to respond after the prompt has been given.

Trainers need to know what to do in response to each of these five types of responses—that is, when to reinforce, when to prompt, and when to use error correction.

In terms of reinforcement, Striefel et al. (1974) provided both an edible reinforcer and social praise as consequences for either type of correct response (i.e., correct anticipations and correct waits). However, once the learner made a correct response to the verbal instruction only, any subsequent correct waits (i.e., correct responses that occurred after the prompt) were reinforced with social praise only. Such differential reinforcement may be useful in producing a quicker transfer of stimulus control. Indeed, in this study, transfer of stimulus control was rapid in that it occurred for all learners on the first trial when a delay of 0.5 second was in effect. However, after being trained to respond to the verb + noun instruction "Push car," the learner would push the car even if the actual instruction was something different, such as "Drop car." The responses, therefore, seem to have come under the control of particular elements of the instruction (i.e., the noun) rather than the complete instruction (i.e., verb + noun).

Smeets and Striefel (1976a) also demonstrated the effectiveness of progressive time delay in teaching a girl who was developmentally disabled and deaf. They sought to teach her to respond to manual color signs made by the trainer. First, the learner was taught to point to a color card identical to the one presented by the trainer (i.e., imitation trial). Next, she was taught to point to the correct color card in the presence of an identical card presented simultaneously with the manual sign for that color (i.e., simultaneous trial). On the final step, she pointed at the correct color card when presented with the manual color sign and before the identical color card was presented (i.e., delay trial); for example, she pointed to the red card when the trainer made the manual sign for "red." The procedure was effective in transferring stimulus control in that the child came to make the correct response without having to be prompted by being shown the identical color card. The new response generalized to another trainer and to other shapes of the same color. Smeets and Striefel (1976b) used the same time-delay procedure to transfer stimulus control from a picture to manual signing when teaching receptive and expressive language responses.

Kohl, Wilcox, and Karlan (1978) employed the progressive time-delay procedure to teach 3 learners with developmental disabilities to sign the correct label for pictures of food items in response to the trainer's spoken and signed question, "What is this?" First, the trainer modeled the correct sign, and if the learner did not imitate the sign, the trainer used physical guidance to prompt the correct response. The trainer then inserted a progressive time delay between demonstrating the sign and providing physical guidance, and then between the simultaneously spoken and signed instruction and the model. The procedure was effective in shifting stimulus control from physical guidance to the model to the spoken and signed instruction, and it was effective across two different trainers in two different situations and with a number of different items.

As the Kohl et al. (1978) study illustrates, teaching learners to use signs or other communicative gestures to convey messages to others is one skill area that seems to lend itself particularly well to the progressive time delay procedure. In the context of teaching functional communication skills, one purpose of progressive time delay is to transfer control of the learner's newly acquired communication responses from instructional prompts, such as physical guidance, models, or specific instructions (e.g., "Sign drink"), to more natural cues, such as the presence of an object or a more natural query from the trainer (e.g., "What do you want?"). This procedure is rather complicated, so we advise the reader to carefully review Table 2.1 and the flowchart in Figure 2.1 (see also Duker, 1988).

In Figure 2.1, the old instruction (Oi) refers to the instructional prompt that already controls the learner's response. The controlling instructional prompt could be a specific verbal instruction ("Sign drink"), a demonstration of the manual sign by the trainer, or perhaps the presentation of the actual object or a picture of the object. The new instruction (Ni), however, will always be the same in this phase of training. The instruction is the trainer's more general query, "What do you want?" Initially, the trainer presents the new instruction ("What do you want?") and the old instruction ("Sign drink") simultaneously or as close in time as possible. This is indicated by the term *0-sec delay*, meaning there is a 0-second delay between the old instruction and the new instruction. The trainer first says, "What do you want?" and then says the old verbal instruction ("Sign drink") to prompt the learner to make one of the manual signs in the learner's repertoire. That is, if the learner has the signs for "drink," "food," and "toy," then the trainer might say, "Sign drink," "Sign food," or "Sign toy."

TABLE 2.1

Progressive Time-Delay Procedure

Step	Trainer Instructions	Response and Result
1	Give new instruction: "What do you want?" Wait 0 seconds. Give old instruction: "Do ..."	Incorrect response: Return to Phase 3 of training (Figure 1.4). Correct response: Reward and proceed to Step 2.
2	Give new instruction: "What do you want?" Wait 2 seconds. Give old instruction: "Do ..."	Incorrect response: Return to Step 1. Correct response: Reward and proceed to Step 3.
3	Give new instruction: "What do you want?" Wait 4 seconds. Give old instruction: "Do ..."	Incorrect response: Return to Step 2. Correct response: Reward and proceed to Step 4.
4	Give new instruction: "What do you want?" Wait 6 seconds. Give old instruction: "Do ..."	Incorrect response: Return to Step 3. Correct response: Reward and proceed to Step 5.
5	Give new instruction: "What do you want?" Wait 10 seconds. Give old instruction: "Do ..."	
6	Stop procedure when learner responds correctly with 10-second delay 3 times in a row.	

Note. Adapted from *Teaching the Developmentally Handicapped Communicative Gesturing: A How-To-Do Book*, by P. Duker, 1988, Berwyn, PA: Swets North American. Copyright 1988 by Swets North American.

Reinforcement (e.g., drink, food, or toy) is given whenever the correct response occurs, even if the response is prompted, at least during the initial stages of training using the time-delay procedure. Unless responses are reinforced in this way, they will not come under the control of the instructional prompt, and so it will not be possible to transfer control to the new instruction in subsequent steps of the training.

As noted before, in the progressive time-delay procedure shown in Table 2.1 and Figure 2.1, a 0-second delay refers to

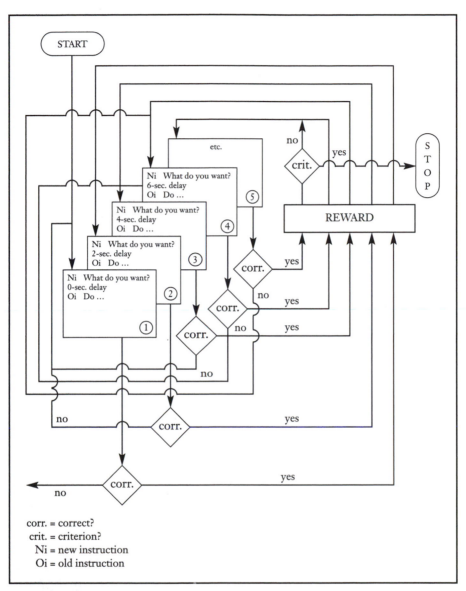

Figure 2.1. Flowchart of the progressive time-delay procedure. *Note.* From *Teaching the Developmentally Handicapped Communicative Gesturing: A How-To-Do Book*, by P. Duker, 1988, Berwyn, PA: Swets North American. Copyright 1988 by Swets North American. Reprinted with permission.

the initial step when the old and new instructions are presented simultaneously or as close in time as possible. That is, initially the time interval between the new and old instructions is as close to 0 seconds as possible. If the learner makes the correct response, then a 2-second delay is inserted between the new and old instructions on the next trial. The trainer says, "What do you want?" and then waits 2 seconds before saying "Sign drink," for example. The best way to count out the time interval is to actually count silently: "one Mississippi, two Mississippi," and so on. If the learner makes an error or does not respond, it is clear that the old instruction is no longer an effective prompt for the response and other instructional prompts need to be added. This means returning to the previous training phase shown in Figure 1.4.

Researchers have not yet discovered the optimal time interval between the new and the old instruction, and this will in fact vary from learner to learner and from task to task. When a trainer is first learning how to implement this procedure, we recommend using the 2-second delay interval as the standard. Data from Duker, van Deursen, de Wit, and Palmen (1997) suggest that this interval is likely to be a good starting point.

After gaining some experience, a trainer will start to recognize when to wait longer and when to provide less of a delay based on the learner's behavior during training. Some learners may need more time to initiate a response because of poor motor coordination. Others, those who are likely to make an impulsive error, will benefit from a shorter delay interval.

Returning to the flowchart in Figure 2.1, the trainer now has reached the second rectangle, indicated by the circled number 2. Here is where the trainer starts to introduce differential reinforcement. Tangible reinforcement related to the response (e.g., the drink, food, or toy) is given for correct responses that occur before the old instruction. If the response does not occur until the old instruction is given, then the trainer gives only verbal praise. This differential reinforcement provides the incentive for the learner to respond earlier during the delay interval rather than wait to be prompted.

Each correct response leads to a 2-second increase in the delay interval, as indicated by the move to 4-second delay and 6-second delay in the third and fourth rectangles of Figure 2.1.

The lengthening intervals make it more efficient for the learner to respond during the delay interval than to wait for the prompt, because the delay is even longer. If the learner makes an incorrect response or does not respond during the delay interval, then the trainer gives the old instruction at the end of the delay interval and, in addition, decreases the delay interval for the next trial by 2 seconds. The general rule is to increase the interval when the learner is correct and to decrease it when the learner makes an incorrect response or no response. After the learner gives three consecutive correct responses to the trainer's question, "What do you want?" the trainer can stop the delay procedure because the learner has reliably responded to the new instruction. Training is considered complete at this stage, but training can be initiated to teach new responses.

Constant time delay is similar to progressive time delay except that the length of the delay before presenting the prompt is always the same. With constant time delay, the prompt is presented after a specified time interval has passed (e.g., 3 or 5 or maybe even 10 seconds). This interval remains constant across the trials and sessions until the acquisition criteria have been attained and transfer of stimulus control achieved. Both progressive and constant time-delay procedures have been effective for achieving transfer of stimulus control. Studies involving constant time delay have used a variety of delay intervals, including 4-, 5-, 10-, and 15-second delays. Studies involving progressive time delay have typically used delay increments of 0.5, 1, or 2 seconds following each correct unprompted or correct prompted response.

An important issue to consider with the time-delay procedure is when to increase the delay interval. In Figure 2.1 the interval is increased with each correct response, but other researchers have applied different decision rules that were also effective. Stremel-Campbell, Cantrell, and Halle (1977), for example, required 90% correct responding over two consecutive 10-trial blocks prior to increasing the delay interval. Braam and Poling (1983) required 15 consecutive correct responses before increasing the delay interval. Advantages and disadvantages may be associated with these varying decision rules, but the potential advantages and disadvantages have not yet been clearly articulated or empirically validated.

In one relevant study, Steele (1977) reported that rapidly increasing the delay interval resulted in quicker transfer of stimulus control, whereas moving more slowly from one delay interval to the next led to a more drawn out transfer process. For some learners, then, it might be better to increase the delay interval after each correct response than to wait for a number of correct responses to occur before increasing the delay interval.

Error correction is another issue that the trainer must learn how to address when using time-delay procedures. Error correction in this context involves two main considerations. The first is how to immediately respond to the learner's error. The trainer can correct errors by prompting a correct response as the learner begins to make an error or by introducing a negative consequence contingent upon an error, such as withdrawing trainer attention for a short period of time. Other error correction procedures that have been used include physical guidance or some other instructional prompt to ensure that the correct response occurs. Another error correction procedure is to momentarily hold the learner's hand, withdraw the materials, and terminate the trial. With this procedure, the next trial is also delayed for a set period of time, perhaps 10 seconds. This procedure is technically known as nonexclusionary timeout. Another way to deal with errors is to repeat the trial until a correct response occurs (Touchette, 1971).

The second main consideration involves changing the length of the delay interval. The progressive time-delay procedure (see Table 2.1 and Figure 2.1) is based on a decision rule that leads to reducing the interval by 2 seconds for each error. Other studies reset the delay length to 0 seconds or to that of the previous trial following an incorrect response. Many factors need to be considered when using time-delay procedures. As a trainer gains experience, he or she should be able to modify the procedures in light of the learner's performance.

There are three potential difficulties in using time delay. The first is the requirement that the target response is already under the control of some stimulus, such as a model or demonstration of the manual sign that is being taught. In cases involving motor responses, such as producing a manual sign or selecting a graphic symbol from an augmentative communication device, the trainer can prompt the learner's response by using physical guidance. Then the trainer can shift control from physical guidance to the model by fading the amount of physical guidance, as was described in Chapter 1. In addition to fading the amount of physical guidance, the trainer can insert a delay between the model and the physical prompt using the procedures shown in Figure 2.1. However, it may not be possible to use physical guidance to prompt some responses, such as a vocal response or eye contact. In cases where the response cannot be prompted, the trainer may need to resort to the often more lengthy process of waiting for approximations of the response to occur and then reinforcing successive approximations of the target behavior. This procedure, known as response shaping, is discussed later in this chapter.

The second potential difficulty occurs when a learner fails to respond during the delay interval and, therefore, always has to be prompted. In such cases, transfer of stimulus control will not occur. It may be helpful to present more trials in which the old and new instructions are presented simultaneously (i.e., with a 0-second delay) before inserting any delay between the new and old instructions; that is, it may help to stay on the 0-second delay step for a longer period of time before moving to the 2-second delay.

The third difficulty occurs when the learner makes errors during the delay interval, before the old instructional prompt is given. There may be many reasons for these errors, some of which can be dealt with effectively by using the error correction procedures described previously. Snell and Kneedler (1978) described a failure in getting two women with severe disabilities to match shapes, letters, and colors using a time-delay procedure. The researchers hypothesized that the failure resulted because the two learners often failed to look at the matching and choice stimuli. In addition, these two learners seemed to respond by always going for a particular position (left or right). This is known as position-biased responding. In these situations, other types of troubleshooting strategies are needed. For example, the trainer may need (a) to first teach the learner to attend to (i.e., look at and scan) the stimuli before responding; (b) to randomly change the position of the stimuli rather than merely always placing them in a left-to-right orientation; or (c) to use differential reinforcement more precisely by making sure that correct unprompted responses receive highly pre-ferred reinforcers and prompted responses are not reinforced.

GRADUATED GUIDANCE

Graduated guidance is a variation of the most-to-least prompt-ing procedure (see Chapter 1). With this type of procedure, the trainer gradually reduces the amount of physical guidance as the learner's performance improves. During the initial few trials, the trainer might, for example, place his or her hand over the learner's hand(s) and physically assist the learner to make the target response. Physical assistance in this case in-volves using the least amount of hand-over-hand guidance that is needed to ensure that the desired response occurs with no possibility for error. Later, as the learner begins to make the movements in concert with the trainer, and therefore starts to respond independently, the trainer begins to provide less and less physical guidance. As progress continues, the trainer might merely rest his or her fingers on the back of the learner's hand, or touch the learner's wrist, or merely tap the learner's elbow until ultimately the learner needs no physical guidance of any kind. If the learner stops responding at any point during the movement, the degree of physical guidance is increased. Gradu-ated guidance is, therefore, a method of giving physical guid-ance that is responsive to and varies with the learner's develop-ing independence in responding.

Graduated guidance can be faded by changing the loca-tion of where the trainer touches the learner to physically prompt a response. Azrin, Schaeffer, and Wesolowski (1976) and Diorio and Konarski (1984) taught adults with profound disabilities to dress themselves using graduated guidance. The guidance was faded by moving the location of the physical prompt from the adults' hands to a forearm, an elbow, a bicep, a shoulder, and finally the upper back.

In addition to fading physical guidance by altering the lo-cation of the prompt, fading can also occur by reducing the intensity or amount of the prompt. With this approach, the trainer continues to deliver the prompt to the same location but reduces the magnitude or intensity of pressure of the prompt across trials. At some point, the intensity is faded to that of merely shadowing the response. With shadowing, the trainer closely mimics the learner's movement within a couple of centimeters but does not actually touch the learner.

The issue of which approach to take in fading physical guidance—that is, by location fading or by intensity fading— may depend on the situation. If the learner knows what to do but cannot sufficiently control the motor aspects of the response with accuracy or fluency, then intensity fading and shadowing may be indicated over location fading. This is particularly true when the learner has difficulty with fine motor control. In contrast, if the learner knows what to do but lacks the motivation to respond or is waiting to be prompted because this requires less initiation and effort, then the use of location fading is indicated.

Graduated guidance differs from other prompting procedures in that it requires the trainer to adjust the amount of prompting from moment to moment depending on the learner's responsiveness to the prompt. The trainer provides graduated guidance at the level required until the learner makes the response, and then the trainer immediately reinforces the response. It may also help to provide ongoing praise when using graduated guidance to encourage the learner's active participation and cooperation.

In a classic study, Azrin and Armstrong (1973) used the graduated guidance procedure with location fading to transfer stimulus control from physical prompts to the natural cues. In this study, 11 learners with profound disabilities were taught to feed themselves. Initially, the trainer provided complete hand-over-hand physical guidance to move the learners through the required motions of self-feeding. As a learner started to show less resistance and some anticipation of the required motor movements, the trainer progressively reduced the physical prompt to a gentle touch of the hand. With greater independent performance, the locus of the guidance was then faded to the arm, followed by the forearm, elbow, bicep, shoulder, and upper back, respectively. The trainer administered only enough physical guidance to initiate a response or to interrupt an error. Praise was provided throughout each training trial regardless of the level of guidance. Eventually no prompting was required and the learners independently fed themselves when presented with their food, which was the natural cue to begin eating.

RESPONSE DELAY

Impulsive responding is characteristic of many learners with developmental disabilities. Impulsive responding refers to the tendency to respond before actually attending to the task. As one would expect, impulsivity increases the likelihood of errors. Trainers must, therefore, know how to teach the learner to attend to a task before responding to reduce impulsive responding and thereby prevent errors. Prevention of impulsivity should also lead to a more rapid acquisition of the desired response. One procedure that can be used to reduce impulsive responding is known as response delay. This procedure involves having the learner wait a short period of time before responding to the task. Response delay, which is really a type of instructional prompt, has received little attention in the training literature.

Lowry and Ross (1975) were the first to demonstrate the effectiveness of the response-delay procedure. They used the procedure in the context of teaching children with severe disabilities to perform a two-color discrimination task. The trainer used a verbal instruction (e.g., "Peter, touch red") but held the colors about 120 cm out of the learner's reach for 5 seconds before moving them closer so that the learner could point to the correct color. The authors hypothesized that a delay would give the learner the opportunity to attend to the task and scan the two choices before making a response, which in turn would increase the likelihood of a correct response. The authors found that the response-delay strategy was associated with significantly lower error rates when compared to a condition during which the learner was allowed to respond immediately following the instruction.

Dyer, Christian, and Luce (1982) replicated these effects in a study involving 3 children with autism. In this study, a response delay was created by holding the child's hands for 3 to 5 seconds following the verbal instruction. The child was asked to respond to the trainer's questions by pointing (e.g., "Point to the doll's head") or by answering questions verbally. For all 3 children, the response-delay condition was more effective than a no-delay condition in terms of correct responding.

In another study, Duker, van Doeselaar, and Verstraten (1993) demonstrated that response delay was more effective than the no-delay condition when teaching communicative gestures. In this study, response delay consisted of holding the learner's hands for 4 seconds during the presentation of the training instruction and then releasing the hands to allow the learner to respond. The authors also found that if the instruction was repeated immediately before the release of the learner's hands, the learner made fewer errors.

Although it is unclear why this procedure works, Meichenbaum and Goodman (1971) speculated that response delay serves to "bring a ... child's overt behavior under his own verbal discriminative control" (p. 124). Impulsive responding may explain why some learners make poor progress during training. Trainers should, therefore, consider the use of the response-delay procedure when teaching learners who respond impulsively during training.

STIMULUS PROMPTING

Response prompts and stimulus prompts can be viewed along a continuum. At one end are response prompts directed at the learner's physical actions, such as physically guiding the learner to make a manual sign. At the other end of the continuum are stimulus prompts, which involve alterations of the stimulus that set the occasion for the target behavior. Prompts can also be distinguished according to whether they are presented before or after the opportunity to respond—in other words, according to whether they are presented either to the stimulus side or to the response side of the instructional trial.

Stimulus prompting procedures involve the gradual change of instructional stimuli in a systematic manner. This process is also referred to as stimulus fading. A stimulus is initially presented in a form that the learner will reliably respond to without errors. For example, the learner might always say "cat" when shown a picture of a cat but never say "cat" when shown the printed word "cat." Across training trials the picture of the cat is then gradually altered so that it becomes the printed word. The goal of stimulus prompting is, therefore, to gradually transfer stimulus control from a stimulus to which the learner will respond correctly to another stimulus, which should control the same response.

For example, the goal of a training program might be to teach a learner to request a cookie by pointing to a graphic symbol showing a line drawing of a cookie. The learner might come to the task with the ability to point to a box that contains her preferred brand of cookies. Stimulus prompting and fading could then be used to transform the cookie box into a symbol for cookies. This process would involve a number of steps. First, the box is placed in view, and when the learner reaches out and touches the full box, a small piece of a cookie is given as a reinforcer. Next, an empty cookie box is presented, and again when the learner touches it, she is given another small piece of cookie. Third, the box is trimmed away until only the product logo of the box remains. The learner touches the logo and receives a cookie. This logo may then become part of a communication board as a means of requesting cookies, spontaneously or in response to the trainer's question, "What do you want?" In this example, stimulus fading is used to transfer stimulus control of the learner's response of reaching for and touching the real cookie box to a much smaller representation of the logo from the box.

Other stimulus prompts, such as adding a picture to a printed word or enhancing and exaggerating features of a graphic symbol, may be faded by gradually decreasing the visibility of the picture or by reducing or removing the exaggerated features of the picture. For example, a stimulus prompting procedure could be used to transfer stimulus control from a graphic symbol that includes both a line drawing and the corresponding printed word to one that consists only of the printed word, thus teaching a learner to read printed words.

Hoogeveen and colleagues (Hoogeveen, Smeets, & Lancioni, 1989; Hoogeveen, Smeets, & van der Houven, 1987) assessed the efficacy of such a program for teaching basic reading skills to children with moderate developmental disabilities. The program consisted of six phases, arranged in a forward chain (see Chapter 3). Phase 1 consisted of four steps. Step 1 was designed to establish imitative control of the required verbalizations. The verbalizations consisted of two components, a self-cueing response, which involved prolonging the sound associated with the object (e.g., "ssss" for snake), followed by a repetition of the initial sound (i.e., "S" for *snake*). Figure 2.2 shows examples of the stimulus materials used in the Hoogeveen et al. (1987) study. As shown, the materials included a picture of a known object with an embedded letter. The letter represents a sound associated with the object. For example, in Figure 2.2 the letter *s* is embedded in a picture of a snake because *snake* is pronounced with a "ssss" sound. Next, the letter *r* is embedded in a picture of a drill because a drill makes a "rrrr" sound. Similarly, the letter *h* is embedded in the picture of a dog breathing heavily because the "hhhh" sound is associated with a panting dog. Finally, the letter *f* is embedded in a picture of a bicycle pump, which makes a "ffff" sound.

On each trial, the trainer showed a card, then named the portrayed object while prolonging the associated sound. This prolongation of the sound was the self-cueing response (e.g., "ssss" for the letter *s*). The trainer then also repeated the sound normally by saying the name of the letter (e.g., "S"). The

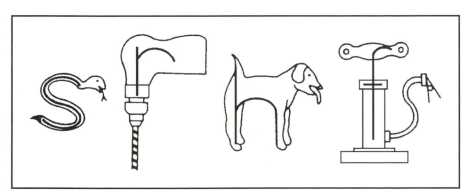

Figure 2.2. Examples of stimulus materials used in a stimulus prompt study. *Note.* From "Establishing Letter–Sound Correspondences in Children Classified as Trainable Mentally Retarded," by F. Hoogeveen, P. M. Smeets, and J. E. van der Houven, 1987, *Education and Training in Mental Retardation, 22,* pp. 77–84. Copyright 1987 by the Division on Mental Retardation, the Council for Exceptional Children. Reprinted with permission.

prolonged sound was to serve as a way for the learner to cue him- or herself to make the correct response, which was to say the name of the letter. This is why it is called a self-cueing response. Five correct imitations of each of these modeled responses were required to attain criterion.

Step 2 was designed to transfer the control of the verbal prompts (i.e., modeled responses) to the visual prompts (i.e., pictures). The learner had to emit the same responses in the presence of the visual cues, but without the assistance of modeling. Criterion was attained when the learner responded correctly on 10 consecutive trials for each picture card in the set.

Step 3 was aimed at shifting control from the picture prompts to the letters. Figure 2.3 shows the gradual reduction,

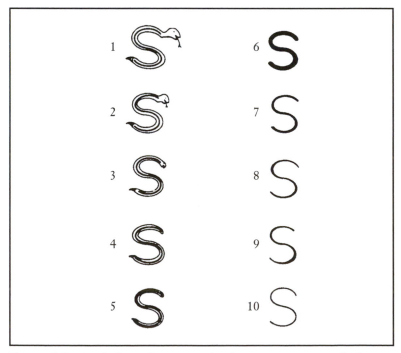

Figure 2.3. Gradual transformation of snake picture prompt to the letter *s*. *Note.* From "Establishing Letter–Sound Correspondences in Children Classified as Trainable Mentally Retarded," by F. Hoogeveen, P. M. Smeets, and J. E. van der Houven, 1987, *Education and Training in Mental Retardation, 22,* pp. 77–84. Copyright 1987 by the Division on Mental Retardation, the Council for Exceptional Children. Reprinted with permission.

through 10 steps, of the pictorial elements while the embedded letter remains unaltered.

Step 4 was directed at teaching the learners to emit only the appropriate sounds. Learners were no longer allowed to make the self-cueing response. For example, when requested to read "S," the learners had to respond with "S" rather than with "ssss" (the self-cueing response). The systematic and gradual changes were designed to make sure the learner made the same correct response as the stimulus was altered.

Several factors must be examined when considering the use of stimulus prompting procedures. Both the targeted response and the stimuli that will be included as part of the instruction will determine, to a great extent, whether a stimulus prompting strategy is appropriate. For example, when teaching communicative gestures, a response prompting procedure might be preferable to a stimulus prompting procedure because the forms or topographies of the gestures being taught are not always the same. The learner needs to be taught to make one form or topography to request a cookie but another to request a drink. Conversely, training that focuses on selecting graphic symbols seems more appropriate for stimulus prompting procedures, because the form of the response for selecting the symbol (e.g., pointing) is the same whether one is selecting a symbol of a cookie or a symbol of a drink. Similarly, responses that are difficult to physically prompt, such as reading a printed word, seem better suited to stimulus prompting, provided that some relevant stimulus (e.g., a picture of a cat) is already effective in evoking the correct spoken word from the learner (e.g., saying "cat").

A variation of stimulus prompting has been used when teaching self-initiated toileting. With this procedure the learner is given liquid to drink at the beginning of the training session (e.g., Duker, Averink, & Melein, 2001). Self-initiated urination cannot be evoked by response prompting procedures alone, so the trainer must try to increase the probability that the response will occur by increasing pressure on the bladder, which is accomplished by getting the person to drink some water or other beverage. Drinking a beverage is thus a type of stimulus prompt. The idea is to teach the learner to feel the pressure on the bladder because this is the natural cue for self-initiated toileting.

Although stimulus prompting is a powerful instructional procedure, a response prompt may also be needed if the learner fails to respond to a stimulus prompt. In addition, response prompts may be needed to correct errors because stimulus prompting strategies do not always prevent or minimize errors. Thus, when designing a training program that includes stimulus prompting, response prompts usually have to be incorporated as well (see Hoogeveen et al., 1989).

Stimulus prompting procedures are easier to use when the stimuli can be easily manipulated in some systematic way. Stimulus prompting strategies are not recommended for situations in which the stimuli are difficult or impractical to alter. For example, it may be time consuming and potentially costly to construct cards with a graphic symbol (e.g., a picture of a cat) that is gradually altered into a printed word (e.g., the printed word "cat").

When planning stimulus prompts, trainers also need to consider the number of steps or levels to use in transforming one stimulus into another. Another issue is that of deciding when to move from one level to the next. Although stimulus prompting procedures produce few errors if the progression from one level to the next is sufficiently gradual, too slow a movement or too many steps may lead to boredom for the learner, increase training time, and slow down the acquisition process. Going too slowly may also result in escape and avoidance behavior (see Chapter 5). Figure 2.3 shows 10 steps to progress from the picture of the snake to the printed letter "S." It is possible, however, that five steps would have been sufficient. On the other hand, going too quickly or having too big a change from one level to the next is likely to increase errors, which can cause emotional outbursts.

There are no hard-and-fast rules for these types of decisions. Much will depend on the nature of the task and the materials, and most important, the learner's performance. Therefore, the trainer needs to monitor the learner's behavior during the progression from level to level to ensure that progress is being made yet errors remain low. If errors increase after moving to the new next level, this is a clear sign that the degree of stimulus change between the levels has become too large and more gradual steps should be taken.

RESPONSE SHAPING

Response shaping refers to a procedure in which the trainer reinforces responses that approximate a certain target response and extinguishes responses that differ from that target response and from previously reinforced approximations. Response shaping is used when the response cannot be prompted. Skills such as eye contact, verbal imitation, and voice loudness may need to be taught using response shaping because such skills are often difficult to prompt. Response shaping requires a great deal of skill and moment-to-moment decision making on the part of the trainer. Initially, the criteria for when to reinforce should be quite lenient to keep the learner active and cooperative. This also increases the probability that the learner will make responses, some of which will be closer approximations of the final desired form of the target response. Because closer approximations are reinforced and less approximate forms are ignored, the probability is increased that even closer approximations of the target response will be made. At this point the criteria for reinforcement can become more stringent.

Haavik and Altman (1977) used a combination of response shaping, response prompting, and forward chaining (see Chapter 3) to teach nonambulatory children with severe disabilities to walk. Table 2.2 illustrates the four training levels for shaping walking.

BEHAVIOR CHAIN INTERRUPTION

The following chain of events leads to eating a bowl of soup: (a) being hungry, (b) going to the cupboard and getting a can of soup, (c) opening the can with a can opener, (d) pouring the soup into a pot, (e) heating the soup, (f) pouring the soup in the bowl, (g) getting a spoon, and (h) using the spoon to eat the soup. In this chain of events, the spoon is a conditioned reinforcer because it is necessary for eating soup. If a spoon is not immediately available, the learner could obtain a spoon by asking, that is, by making a request. When communicative requests are taught within such extended behavior chains, learners must first know that a spoon is needed to eat the soup. In

TABLE 2.2
Description of the Four Training Levels for Shaping Walking

Objectives	Methodology
Level I	
Given a trainer holding one hand, the learner takes alternating steps in a forward direction. Criterion is an average of 5 to 25 steps per 10-trial session for 3 sessions.	Have the learner walk a few steps holding the trainer's hand. As the learner gains skill, the distance the learner has to walk to obtain the positive consequence is gradually increased.
Level II	
Given a rope (one end held by a trainer and the other by the learner), the learner takes alternating steps in a forward direction. Criterion is an average of 15 to 25 steps per 10-trial session for 3 sessions.	Have the learner grasp several thicknesses of taut rope, with the trainer's hand directly adjacent to the learner's hand. Then, the length of the rope between the trainer and the learner is gradually increased to a maximum of 12 to 18 inches. As the learner gains skill, the thickness of the rope is decreased. Initially the rope is held taut; later the trainer can slacken the rope, thereby allowing the learner a momentary experience of independent walking. In this way, support by the taut rope can be alternated with increasingly longer periods of the slackened rope following a schedule dictated by the learner's level of acquisition.
Level III	
The learner is placed in the standing position and takes independent alternating steps in a forward direction. Criterion is an average of 15 to 25 steps per 10-trial session for 3 sessions.	After placing the learner in a standing position, have the learner walk to an attractive positive consequence. Gradually increase the distance the learner must walk. A large, open environment should be selected with no intervening physical barrier that would reduce the probability of the learner's walking the maximum distance.

(continues)

addition, the need for communication must be created by either blocking access to one of the required objects or removing a needed object. For example, the trainer could momentarily interrupt the learner's access to an object that is needed to

TABLE 2.2 *Continued.*

Objectives	Methodology
Level IV	
At random periods during a session when given a verbal or visual cue, the learner will initiate independent walking toward an attractive object and/or when verbally instructed to walk. Criterion is an average of 80% success per 10 trials for 3 sessions. Crawling or other nonwalking modes of ambulation constitute an unsuccessful trial.	The environment should be arranged so that attractive and/or necessary objects are far enough from the learner to require walking. Placing objects higher makes crawling less functional. Crawling should be stopped immediately if it occurs and followed by placement of the learner in the standing position and a short physical prompt to initiate walking. A successful trial is immediately followed by a positive consequence.

Note. From "Establishing Walking in Severely Retarded Children," by S. Haavik and K. Altman, 1977, *Perceptual and Motor Skills, 44*, pp. 1107–1114. Copyright 1977 by Perceptual and Motor Skills. Reprinted with permission.

complete the chain. In this procedure, the object to be requested may be visible when the interruption procedure is used, providing a supplemental cue for what to request.

Halle, Marshall, and Spradlin (1979) taught learners with developmental disabilities to request meals in a cafeteria. The chain of events consisted of (a) getting to the cafeteria counter, (b) picking up a tray, (c) obtaining the food, and (d) taking the meal to a table to eat. The trainer interrupted this chain by blocking access to the cafeteria trays. At the point of interruption, the trainer modeled the correct request, which was to say, "Tray please." The model was faded using a constant time-delay procedure. In addition, the trays were visible to the learners, which may have provided an additional cue for responding. The procedure was effective in teaching the learners to request the required tray.

In another example of the use of behavior chain interruption, a trainer interrupts a learner from going outside to play by momentarily blocking the learner's passage through the door. The trainer's action sets the occasion for the learner to make an appropriate request, such as "Can I go outside?" In a variation of this procedure, called the missing-item format, the trainer withholds a needed item until the learner requests it. For example, a learner may find that his preferred puzzle has some pieces missing. This sets the occasion to request the missing parts. Duker, Kraaykamp, and Visser (1994) demonstrated the effectiveness of this procedure with 6 children with severe to profound disabilities.

These examples of using the behavior chain interruption strategy are meant to illustrate how the daily setting can become a powerful context for teaching. It is important to remember that when using behavior chain interruption, the trainer may also need to use other response or stimulus prompting procedures.

CUES–PAUSE–POINT

Echolalia is characteristic of individuals with autism. Echolalia refers to the immediate or delayed repetition of one or more words or even a sentence uttered, for example, by a parent or teacher. This tendency to echo the speech of others hinders efforts to teach functional communication skills. Cues–pause–point is a procedure that can be used to replace echolalia with functional speech. In a one-to-one training format, the trainer can exploit the learner's tendency to echo in order to prompt a desired response. For example, the trainer shows a child a toy car and asks, "What is this?" Instead of waiting for the child to answer, however, the trainer immediately says, "car." The echolalic child is likely to repeat the response, "car." The trainer's verbal cue ("What is this?") is followed by a verbal model ("car"), which is used as a response prompt, and this prompt is initially given after a 0-second delay. The trainer then fades the verbal model by speaking the word "car" with less and less volume and emphasis as the child continues to respond with the correct answer. In effect, the trainer is fading the intensity of the verbal model prompt. The process continues until the trainer is no longer speaking the verbal model prompt.

Although the effectiveness of this procedure has been demonstrated in many studies, a learner may fail to make the correct response when the prompt has been withdrawn completely. To overcome this problem, McMorrow and Foxx (1986) designed a procedure known as cues–pause–point. This procedure requires that the learner be able to verbally label the pictures or objects involved in the training. During training, the trainer prompts the learner to remain silent before, during, and briefly after the instructional question (e.g., "What is this?"). In this respect the procedure is similar to response delay. In cues–pause–point, the trainer follows five steps. First, the trainer makes the pause prompt by holding his or her right finger at eye level midway between the learner and trainer to prompt silence, and by saying "No" or "Shh" when a verbalization occurs. Second, the trainer moves the finger to touch the correct cue (i.e., a photo or object) approximately 2 seconds after asking, "What is this?" Third, the photo or object is covered with a folder and the trainer uses a bridging stimulus (i.e., a head nod or smile) immediately after the learner's labeling response. Fourth, the trainer gives the pause prompt again, restates the question, and moves his or her right index finger so that it touches the folder when a correct response is desired. Fifth, the trainer provides verbal feedback and consequences for the verbalization that occurs. As may be clear from this description, this is a fairly complicated procedure that may require much practice for the trainer to master. For more information about the cues–pause–point procedure, see McMorrow, Foxx, Faw, and Bittle (1987) and Foxx, McMorrow, Faw, Kyle, and Bittle (1987).

RESPONSE RESTRICTION

Basic psychological research has shown that physically restricting a person from making one response is often sufficient to increase another response. In applied work, however, it is not clear what response may increase when a specific response is restricted. The response may depend on the other available responses in the learner's behavioral repertoire, the context, the learner's current motivational state, prior history of reinforcement for various response options, and the way in which the response is restricted. Many things can restrict responses. For individuals with developmental disabilities, parents or teachers may impose constraints on some behaviors. It seems highly probable, then, that these individuals will use stereotypic behaviors if other responses are restricted. This possibility needs to be considered before using a response restriction procedure.

Duker et al. (2001) assessed the effect of response restriction in establishing diurnal bladder control in people with developmental disabilities. In the first step of the procedure, the learner stood next to the toilet, while the trainer physically prevented the learner from sitting on the ground or walking more than 30 cm from the toilet. Other responses were also restricted (e.g., putting hands in the toilet bowl, flushing the toilet, stereotypic behaviors), but approximations of the desired response of voiding in the toilet, such as lowering pants and sitting on the toilet, were allowed. To restrict the learner's responses, different markings on the floor indicated the distance from the toilet from which the learner was allowed to move (see Figure 2.4). The different taped markings show increasing distances and hence less restriction as training progressed. In addition to restricting where the learner could be and what the learner could do, the trainer also avoided eye contact and did not speak to the learner. The only thing that the learner could do was to sit on the toilet. Because the learner had been given water to drink prior to the session, urination was highly likely to occur when the learner was sitting on the toilet. Following urination, the learner was reinforced. This procedure has proven to be very effective for toilet training.

IMITATION

Imitation is a form of stimulus control that can be used in training. Imitation involves doing something that another person has modeled. Often a teacher or parent will model a behavior, such as how to open a door, tie a shoe, or spread butter on toast, with the hope that the learner will imitate. Once the learner has acquired imitative abilities, the trainer can teach new responses very quickly by modeling alone. Imitation may also be effective in teaching complex motor responses, such as swimming the breaststroke or practicing a new dance step, provided that the learner is capable of executing the motor responses

Figure 2.4. Photograph showing floor markings that indicated the distance from toilet from which the learner was allowed to move during the response restriction procedure described by Duker et al. (2001).

being modeled and imitative control has already been established. If the learner does not already imitate, however, then other prompting strategies can be used to teach imitation.

In a study involving 3 children with profound disabilities, Baer, Peterson, and Sherman (1967) demonstrated that imitation can be taught as a response. Initially, these 3 learners did not imitate any responses modeled by the trainer. The trainer then used physical guidance and reinforcement to teach them a few simple motor responses, such as raising the left arm, tapping a table, or moving the arm in a circular motion. The trainer provided the natural cue by performing the action and then prompted the learner to do the same action. As the prompts were faded, the children began to do the motor acts to the natural cue of the trainer demonstrating the act. Eventually the learners began to imitate newly modeled actions that had never before been demonstrated, prompted, or reinforced. At this point, the children were said to have learned to imitate in a generalized way.

In a related study, Lovaas, Berberich, Perloff, and Schaeffer (1966) focused on teaching imitation of speech rather than motor responses. This is probably a more difficult response to teach because, unlike raising an arm or clapping one's hands, speech cannot be physically prompted by the trainer. The study involved teaching English words to 2 children with autism in response to these same words' being modeled by the trainer. Then, some Norwegian words were brought into the sequence, without reinforcement. With continued reinforcement of the English words, the children's pronunciations of the Norwegian words gradually improved. These results suggest that there was generalization from English to Norwegian words. Unfortunately, it has proven difficult to obtain this type of generalization from trained to untrained words with learners with more severe disabilities. This difficulty could be due to a number of factors, such as the need to closely attend to the trainer's model and the fact that imitation is a social behavior and some individuals with severe disabilities may not be motivated to participate in social interactions of this type.

COMPARATIVE ANALYSIS OF PROCEDURES

Several studies have sought to compare the relative effectiveness of different procedures for transferring stimulus control. A review of the findings from these studies may assist trainers in selecting an effective procedure when teaching individuals with developmental disabilities. Riley (1993) compared most-to-least and least-to-most prompting procedures in the context of teaching 4 individuals with severe disabilities in a two-choice color discrimination task. In this study, the most-to-least hierarchy consisted of (a) full physical guidance with verbal direction, (b) partial physical guidance, (c) gesture prompt, and (d) verbal instruction. The least-to-most hierarchy consisted of (a) verbal instruction, (b) gesture prompt, (c) partial physical guidance, and (d) full physical guidance. The results showed that the most-to-least hierarchy was associated with better performance in terms of higher rates of correct responses and fewer errors and, therefore, appeared to be the more efficient strategy.

Csapo (1981) also compared most-to-least and least-to-most prompting procedures for teaching learners with severe and profound disabilities to make two-choice discriminations. Learners were presented with two different colored blocks and were asked to give one block to the trainer (e.g., "Give blue"). In the least-to-most prompting condition, the trainer first made a verbal request. If the learner failed to respond correctly, the trainer pointed, then provided partial physical guidance, and then provided full physical guidance until the correct response occurred. In the most-to-least prompting condition, the verbal request was first paired with full physical guidance. After the learner responded correctly three consecutive times at that prompt level, the full physical prompt was faded to partial physical guidance, then to a gesture prompt, and finally to verbal instruction alone. The learners who were trained initially with the most-to-least procedure showed steady increases in correct responding and low error rates. A change to the least-to-most condition resulted in an initial drop in their performance, followed by an increase in correct responding. Correct responses also increased at a faster rate than during the most-to-least condition. In contrast, learners who first received training using least-to-most prompting procedures had higher initial error rates. The results of this study suggest that most-to-least prompting is more effective for the establishment of a response, whereas least-to-most prompting is more effective when the response has been acquired but is not yet under appropriate stimulus control.

Other researchers have compared different procedures. Gast, Ault, Wolery, Doyle, and Belanger (1988), for example, compared the use of constant time delay with least-to-most prompting using a functional sight-word reading task. Specifically, both procedures were used to teach learners with moderate developmental disabilities to read words commonly found in grocery stores. Three learners read out loud using speech, and the fourth used manual signs. During one of the two daily sessions, learners received instruction using the constant time-delay procedure. During the other daily session, least-to-most prompting was used. The constant time-delay procedure consisted of a constant 4-second delay between the natural cue and a verbal or signed model by the trainer. The hierarchy of prompts, within the least-to-most procedure, began with a verbal instruction and proceeded to the verbal instruction plus verbal description of the item, the verbal instruction plus a photograph of the word, and finally a verbal instruction plus a verbal or signed model of the correct response. A 4-second delay also was used between prompt levels in the least-to-most procedure. The procedures were found to be equally effective in teaching functional sight-word reading. In terms of efficiency (as measured by the amount of instructional time needed, the number of sessions to criterion, and percentage of errors), the constant time-delay procedure appeared to be more efficient than the least-to-most prompting procedure.

In another relevant study, Schoen (1986) compared graduated guidance and most-to-least prompting procedures in teaching self-help skills to preschoolers with moderate disabilities. The learners were taught to wash their hands and to drink from a water fountain using the graduated guidance sequence of (a) full graduated guidance, (b) partial graduated guidance (i.e., thumb and forefinger guidance), and (c) verbal direction, and using the most-to-least sequence of (a) physical guidance (i.e., hand-over-hand guidance), (b) modeling, and (c) verbal instruction. Because no significant difference in training time was required to teach the skills across these two instructional procedures, Schoen concluded that both procedures were equally effective.

Ault, Gast, and Wolery (1988) compared progressive and constant time-delay procedures in a study designed to teach functional sight-word reading to 3 learners with moderate disabilities. Each of the two types of time-delay procedures, progressive and constant, was used to teach six words. Progressive time delay consisted of increasing the delay by 1 second between (a) the presentation of a card on which a word was written and the verbal cue "What word?" and (b) the prompt, which consisted of a verbal model of the correct response until an 8-second delay was reached. Both correct unprompted responses (i.e., the learner responded to the verbal cue by reading the word on the card) and correct wait responses (i.e., the learner did not respond during the delay interval but emitted the correct response after the trainer's model) were reinforced. If the learner made an unprompted incorrect response, the trainer corrected the error by instructing the learner to wait for the model, removing the card, and looking away for 10 seconds. Wait errors (i.e., incorrect responses after the trainer's model) and no responses were followed by the trainer's saying "No," removing the card, and looking away for 10 seconds. The constant time-delay procedure involved a 5-second delay between the presentation of the card with the cue ("What word?") and the prompt, which consisted of the trainer's model of the correct response. Correct and incorrect responses were dealt with in the same manner as under the progressive time-delay procedure. The learners reached criterion with both procedures, although the constant time-delay procedure was more efficient in terms of the amount of instructional time and the number of sessions required for the learner to master the words. One of the 3 learners made more errors during the progressive time-delay procedure, whereas another learner made more errors during the constant time-delay procedure, and the third learner showed no difference in this respect.

From an applied perspective, these studies suggest that there may be no major differences in the relative effectiveness of the various prompting procedures. All of the procedures can be effective for teaching skills to individuals with developmental disabilities. Under some conditions or with some learners, one procedure may be slightly more effective than another, but overall such differences may not be of major clinical importance. It should be remembered, however, that these comparative studies have generally involved only small samples of participants. This small sample size precludes us from making any firm statements regarding the effectiveness of one procedure over another.

Therefore, until more evidence is available, perhaps the best advice we can give is that the trainer's choice of one prompting procedure over another should be guided by the response of the learner, characteristics of the task, and abilities of the trainer. Some trainers may find it easier to use constant time delay rather than progressive time delay. As a result, they may be better at implementing a constant time-delay procedure. Due to better implementation, the learner might in fact be expected to learn faster, so this then becomes the more effective procedure. Table 2.3 provides a summary of the charac-

TABLE 2.3

Summary of Characteristics, Advantages, and Disadvantages
of Most-to-Least, Least-to-Most, and Time-Delay Procedures

Procedure	Characteristics	Advantages and Disadvantages
Most to least	Prompts delivered in a sequence from more to less intrusive. Several distinct prompts are included (e.g., physical, model, gesture, verbal).	*Advantages:* Time required to evoke response is minimized, leading to quicker reinforcement. Errors are minimized. *Disadvantages:* May preempt independence.
Least to most	Prompts delivered in a sequence from less to more intrusive. Several distinct prompts are included (e.g., verbal, gesture, model, physical).	*Advantages:* Clear criteria for moving from one prompt level to the next. *Disadvantages:* May be necessary to move through entire sequence, which adds to training time and delays reinforcement. More opportunities for errors.
Time delay	Systematic use of delay before prompting and before moving from one prompt level to the next.	*Advantages:* Creates opportunity for independence to natural cues. *Disadvantages:* Errors may occur during delay. Long delays increase training time and delay reinforcement.

teristics, advantages, and disadvantages of three prompting procedures—most to least, least to most, and time delay—which have been the main focus of comparative studies.

STIMULUS OVERSELECTIVITY

One problem that may arise in teaching people with developmental disabilities is that their behaviors may come under the control of irrelevant stimuli. A trainer may be trying to teach the learner to point to the correct picture to request preferred items, for example, but the learner's pointing response may be controlled by some irrelevant aspect of the picture, such as the color or the border around the picture. This shows up when new pictures with identical colors or borders are introduced and the learner begins to respond at chance levels. This is a problem that trainers need to solve during the training process by making sure that irrelevant stimuli do not coincide with relevant stimuli.

Lovaas and his colleagues (e.g., Lovaas & Schreibman, 1971; Lovaas, Schreibman, Koegel, & Rehm, 1971) studied this phenomenon. In one study, Lovaas and Schreibman (1971) taught 9 children with autism to press a lever in the presence of a complex stimulus consisting of auditory and visual stimuli. When the complex stimulus reliably controlled responding, each of the two components of the complex stimulus was presented separately to test which component had gained control of the response. Some of the children with autism responded to only one of the two stimuli, whereas nondisabled children typically respond correctly to the complex stimulus, the auditory stimulus alone, and the visual stimulus alone. For example, in the Lovaas and Schreibman study, one child showed considerable overselectivity to the auditory stimulus in that he never responded to the visual component when it was presented alone. Another student, in contrast, showed overselectivity to the visual stimulus in that he was less likely to respond to the auditory stimulus alone. These results suggest that children with autism may be overselective in their responding to available stimuli. Lovaas and Schreibman labeled this phenomenon "stimulus overselectivity." This tendency to overselect has been demonstrated in numerous studies with a wide range of children with developmental disabilities.

The identification of stimulus overselectivity and the use of procedures to remediate it is important for a number of reasons. One reason is that stimulus overselectivity could be a contributing factor to behavioral deficits, including impairments in respondent conditioning and observational learning, problems in developing conditioned reinforcers, limitations on certain transfer of stimulus control procedures in training, and limitations on the generalization of training effects (for a review, see Lovaas et al., 1979).

SUMMARY AND CONCLUSION

The range of procedures covered in this chapter complement those described in Chapter 1. This chapter has extended the discussion begun in Chapter 1 by considering transfer of stimulus control procedures in more detail and considering a range of additional procedures for teaching new single-component responses to learners with developmental disabilities. The procedures described in the first two chapters also can be used when teaching multiple-component responses, but in the latter case, the trainer must consider the additional issues that are described in the next chapter.

Chapter 3

◆◆◆◆◆◆◆◆◆◆◆◆◆◆◆◆◆◆◆◆◆◆◆◆◆◆◆◆◆

Multiple-Component Response Training

n the first two chapters, we described instructional procedures for teaching skills that involve a single behavior or response. Included were a description of instructional prompts that are used to ensure that the response occurs and procedures for fading those prompts so that the response comes under the control of natural cues. These same prompting and fading strategies also can be used when the goal is to teach skills that involve more than a single behavior or response. We focused on single responses first because it is useful for the trainer to begin with the goal of teaching a single response, and doing so increases the likelihood that the learner will experience success. As the learner makes progress and the trainer becomes more confident in his or her teaching abilities, then it becomes appropriate and indeed necessary to build up the learner's repertoire by introducing additional and more complicated responses. The aim of this chapter is to describe procedures for teaching more complicated skills that require multiple responses.

THE CONCEPT OF CHAINING

Participation in home, school, vocational, and community settings will require the learner to perform complex skills that involve a sequence of interrelated responses, or a *behavioral chain*. This term indicates that completing the activity or skill requires the learner to complete a chain of responses in the correct order. Examples of behavioral chains include washing dishes, dressing, shopping for groceries, preparing a meal, making a cup of coffee, making a telephone call, repairing a flat tire on a bicycle, washing a car, and waiting on tables in a restaurant. Such tasks—be they domestic, academic, recreational, or vocational—involve either a fixed or a semifixed sequence of interrelated responses. Opening the dishwasher, for example, is related to stacking the dishes inside because the former must by necessity precede the latter. If one response in the chain is not completed or if it is performed incorrectly or out of sequence, then the task cannot be completed. It is important to remember that a behavioral chain consists of a number of responses that are temporally or sequentially and functionally related to one another. That is, a behavioral chain is not an arbitrary sequence of responses.

It is also critical to understand that the individual responses making up a chain have at least three functions. First, the completion of each response in the chain leads to a critical outcome that enables the next response to be performed. Second, completion of one response becomes the natural cue or discriminative stimulus for moving on to the next response. Third, at the completion of the entire sequence, reinforcement arises as a natural consequence of having completed the task. For example, after preparing a meal, the reinforcer is eating what has been prepared. Thus, completing each response in the chain gets the learner closer to the end of the chain; therefore, completion of each step functions as conditioned reinforcement (see Chapter 4).

Teaching learners with developmental disabilities to correctly perform all of the many and varied responses that are necessary to complete a complex activity, such as washing dishes or preparing a meal, may seem daunting at first. Training is easier when the task is broken down into smaller teachable steps. A first step in doing this is to think of the complex task as a chain or series of single responses. Each response is taught separately and then linked to the previous and next response in the chain. In adopting this approach to teaching complex skills, the trainer needs to try to clarify three aspects of the training: (a) the stimuli that should control each response in the behavioral chain, (b) the reinforcing consequence that will occur at the end of the chain, and (c) the instructional procedures (i.e., prompting and fading strategies) that will be used to ensure that each response in the chain is acquired and brought under appropriate stimulus control.

Figure 3.1 provides an example of a response chain for making toast. It begins with three criteria that are present at the start of each training session. First, the learner is hungry and likes to eat toast. Second, all the necessary materials (e.g., bread, toaster, plate, knife, butter) are available. Third, the learner is physically capable of the motor responses that are required to complete each step of the task.

The chain outlined in Figure 3.1 involves four steps, but it is possible, and for some learners necessary, to break these into smaller steps. For example, Step 4 ("Butter toast with knife")

Natural Cue	Response 1	Response 2	Response 3	Response 4	Reinforcer
Breakfast time	Put bread in toaster.	Push lever down.	When toasted, move toast to plate.	Butter toast with knife.	Eat toast.

Figure 3.1. The chain of responses involved in preparing toast for breakfast.

could be broken down into a number of smaller steps, such as (1) pick up knife, (2) scrape butter onto knife, and (3) spread butter onto toast. The act of breaking down a complex task, such as toasting bread, into smaller and more easily teachable steps is known as *task analysis*, which is discussed in the next section of this chapter.

In addition to specifying the responses in the chain, the trainer considers the general instructional approach, which involves three phases. First, each response in the chain is taught separately using the strategies described in Chapters 1 and 2. Second, natural reinforcement is given at the end of the task so that each response leading to completion of the task becomes a conditioned reinforcer. During the initial teaching sessions, instructional reinforcers are delivered for each correct response in the chain in addition to the continued provision of natural reinforcement that occurs at the end of the chain. Ideally, these instructional reinforcers can be faded as each response is acquired, because over time the mere act of completing the response should become a conditioned reinforcer. Third, the separate responses are chained together so that performing one response in the chain produces a change in the configuration of the task, and this change is the discriminative stimulus for initiating the next response in the chain. That is, each separate response in the chain must be controlled by the effect produced by the previous response and maintained by its own effect. As this occurs, the learner eventually completes all steps in the task in their proper sequence.

An important concept is the strength of the chain. A chain is strong when the completion of each response is an effective discriminative stimulus for initiating the next response in the chain so that each response follows the previous one in a fluid manner. The responses should follow one another without obvious delay and without the need for prompting by the trainer. The strength of a chain is indicated by how well early responses in the chain are maintained over time once the instructional reinforcers have been faded.

One of the main goals of multiple-component response training is to develop strong behavioral chains. The strength of any chain is a function of at least three aspects of training: (a) the effectiveness of the procedures that were used to teach each separate response in the chain, (b) the extent to which completion of each response creates a discriminative stimulus for initiating the next response, and (c) the power of the natural reinforcement at the end of the chain.

The more powerful the natural reinforcer at the end of the chain, the more likely it is that the chain will be strong. If at any time the final response in the chain does not result in reinforcement, then the other links in the chains are also weakened. The effects of this nonreinforcement, which is more technically known as extinction, include increased variability of the responses (Duker & van Lent, 1991); emotional outbursts; and an overall decrease in the strength of the chain, especially for early responses in the chain. This may mean that on the next opportunity, the learner fails to initiate the first few responses in the chain. It may appear as if the learner cannot remember where to start. This problem with initiation would be predicted because the strength of the (conditioned) reinforcers in the response chain varies, so that those closest to the natural reinforcer at the end of the chain are the strongest and those at the beginning of the chain are the weakest. The difference in strength from start to finish also depends on the size of the chain. Conditioned reinforcement for the first few responses in a long chain with, for instance, 10 responses will be weaker than if the chain had only 5 responses.

TASK ANALYSIS

As we have already mentioned, many tasks or skills involve multiple responses. Multiple-component response training involves teaching each separate response in the task and combining these separate responses into a behavioral chain. To accomplish this, the trainer must first perform a task analysis—that is, break the task into teachable steps. A task analysis is, therefore, a list of the separate responses, in their proper sequence, that lead to the completion of a specific task. Table 3.1 shows three tasks that have been analyzed into component steps for instructional purposes.

Writing a task analysis for instructional purposes requires a number of important considerations. First, the task analysis needs to be consistent with what might be considered the natural lines of fracture along which the steps of the task break;

TABLE 3.1

Task Analyses for Operating a Vending Machine,
Cooking an Egg, and Washing Clothing

Steps	Operating Vending Machine	Cooking Egg	Washing Clothes
1	Remove correct change from wallet or purse.	Fill 1-quart saucepan ¾ full of water.	Sort clothes by color.
2	Insert coins.	Place pan on stovetop burner at high heat.	Place dark (light) colors in machine.
3	Press panel of desired item.	When water boils, add 2 eggs.	Add 1 cup of detergent.
4	Remove item.	After 5 minutes, remove from heat.	Select desired wash settings.
5	Collect change if applicable.	Drain water and rinse eggs in cold water for 1 minute.	Insert coins.
6	Consume item.	Remove shells and eat.	When the spin cycle ends, remove clothes.

that is, the task analysis should closely match the actual steps involved in the task. It is often difficult to know where these fracture lines should be drawn. Trainers, therefore, should undertake the task themselves while keeping a record of the steps needed to complete the task. In addition, trainers might observe other people performing the task and note their steps. From such experiences and observations, the trainer develops a preliminary task analysis for pilot testing during the instructional program. Because such observations can be time consuming, expensive, and inefficient, especially if the task is prolonged and requires the use of costly materials, trainers instead might peruse the numerous task analyses already published in the professional literature. Among those already proven effective for teaching learners with developmental disabilities are task analyses for teaching laundry skills (McDonnell & McFarland, 1988), toothbrushing (Horner & Keilitz, 1975), mending skills (Cronin & Cuvo, 1979), telephone answering (Karen, Astin-Smith, & Creasy, 1985), and operating a pocket calculator (Smeets & Kleinloog, 1980).

A second important consideration is the size of the steps in the task analysis. It may be unclear whether a particular component of the task should be listed as one big step or as two or more smaller steps. In our example of cooking an egg (in Table 3.1), for example, the act of placing the egg into the saucepan of boiling water is listed as one step, but this could have been expanded into five smaller steps: (1) pick up egg, (2) place egg on wooden spoon, (3) lower wooden spoon into water, (4) roll egg off spoon into water, and (5) remove wooden spoon. There is no correct number or size for steps in a task analysis; the learner's performance during training will determine whether the steps are too many and too small or too few and too large. If a learner is having difficulty learning a specific step, then that step should be reanalyzed and possibly broken into smaller steps. If, on the other hand, the learner proceeds into other steps without any training, the steps are perhaps too small, and the learner's performance can be taken into account when developing future task analyses for this individual. The number and size of steps in a task analysis should conform to the estimated ability of the learner. A skill such as cooking an egg can consist of 6 steps or 16 steps, depending on the trainer's estimate of the learner's performance during or prior to training.

A third consideration involves determining reinforcing consequences for completing each step of the task. Reinforcing consequences are most important during the early stages of training, when the learner's performance has not yet come under the control of conditioned reinforcement. The trainer may need to introduce and continue to use instructional reinforcers in cases where the natural outcome of completing the task is not an effective type of reinforcement for the learner. For instance, the natural outcome of washing clothes is that the person gets clean clothing. But clean clothes may not be a sufficient consequence to maintain the complex chain of responses for some learners with developmental disabilities. These individuals may need instructional reinforcement (e.g., praise, preferred objects, or activities) if they are to learn to wash their clothes and then maintain this skill over time. For example, after completing the task, the learner receives praise and might also get to choose from among several preferred and more tangible options, such as food, drinks, or leisure activities.

A fourth consideration is technical adequacy. When using a task analysis to guide instruction, the trainer needs to specify the desired performance criteria. Each response in the task analysis must be objectively defined so that it is both observable and measurable. In addition, the trainer must specify how well the step must be learned before the learner can move on to the next step. Criteria are often specified in terms of latency (e.g., within 10 seconds of completing the previous step), performance (e.g., 100% correct), and time (e.g., over three consecutive sessions).

Sigafoos and DePaepe (1994) described a format for writing technically adequate goal statements that lends itself to task-analyzed skills. The top box in Figure 3.2 shows an example of the format for the goal of teaching a learner to make a pot of coffee. In this example, the skill is said to be acquired when Jane completes each of the 10 steps correctly and independently (i.e., without prompting) for 10 consecutive days. The lower box in Figure 3.2 is a format for writing behavioral

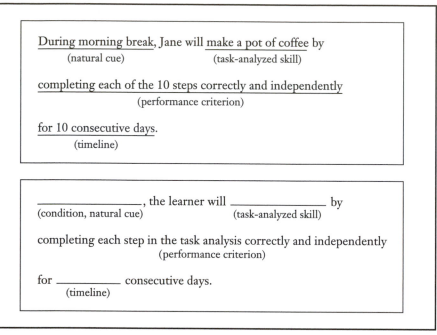

Figure 3.2. Example and format for writing technically adequate goal statements. *Note.* Adapted from "Writing IPP Objectives To Replace Challenging Behaviors with Functional, Age-Appropriate Alternatives," by J. Sigafoos and P. DePaepe, 1994, *Journal of Practical Approaches to Developmental Handicaps, 18*(2), pp. 24–28.

objectives that the trainer completes by writing the details in the blanks. This format can be used for any type of task-analyzed skill, such as washing clothes, preparing a meal, repairing a flat tire, or mailing a letter.

CHAINING PROCEDURES

As we mentioned before, the process of teaching a task that requires multiple responses occurs in stages. First, a task analysis is completed to break the skill into teachable steps. Next, each step of the task or each response in the chain is taught separately. Third, the separate responses need to be linked together to create a strong chain. To link the separate responses into a behavioral chain, three procedures can be used: backward chaining, forward chaining, and total task training.

Backward Chaining

With backward chaining, the separate responses that are required to complete a task are trained one at a time, beginning with the last response in the chain. When the learner has acquired the last response, the second to last response is taught. At this point, the learner is expected to complete both the second to last step and the last step in each training session. When the second to last step is acquired to criterion, the third to last step is added. This means that the learner must do the last three steps in each training session. Training continues in this backward fashion until all steps have been added to the chain. Figure 3.3 illustrates the backward chaining approach.

As shown in Figure 3.3, in Step 1 the trainer teaches the final step of the task (R_n) and then reinforces the learner. The stimulus or cue for the final response (R_n) is indicated by the letter *S* (for *stimulus*). After the learner has acquired the final response in the chain, Step 2 begins in which the learner is taught to also perform the second to last step in the chain ($R_n - 1$). Completing this second to last step produces the stimulus for the final step, which is completed to obtain reinforcement. The process continues until all steps have been added to the chain.

Although backward chaining may seem counterintuitive, it is based on a compelling logic. In a behavioral chain involving several responses, reinforcement comes at the end of the chain when the final response has been made. Focusing initially on the last step means that the learner only has to make

Step	Chains			
1				$S \rightarrow R_n \rightarrow$ Reinforcer
2			$S \rightarrow R_n - 1$	$(S) \rightarrow R_n \rightarrow$ Reinforcer
3		$S \rightarrow R_n - 2 \ (S) \rightarrow R_n - 1$		$(S) \rightarrow R_n \rightarrow$ Reinforcer
N	$S \rightarrow R_n - N \ (S) \longrightarrow R_n - 2 \ (S) \rightarrow R_n - 1$			$(S) \rightarrow R_n \rightarrow$ Reinforcer

Figure 3.3. Schematic representation of backward chaining. *Note.* S = stimulus; R_n = final response; N = number of steps.

one response before reinforcement. This more immediate re-inforcement is important at the early stages of training and is an advantage of the backward chaining approach.

When teaching with this procedure, the trainer starts by completing all the steps except the last step. When the trainer comes to the last step in the task analysis, the trainer pauses and uses the techniques described in Chapters 1 and 2 to teach the learner to do the last step. When the learner completes the last step, even if prompted, then reinforcement occurs. Once this step is acquired, the trainer does all but the last two steps and then teaches the learner to do the second to last step. Completing the second to last step should thus create a discriminative stimulus for performing the last step, which the learner has already acquired, and so the last step should follow without prompting. Completion of the last step, in turn, leads to the reinforcer.

The backward chaining procedure has been used to teach a variety of multiple-component responses, including toileting skills, eating with a spoon and fork, dressing and undressing, and doing leisure activities, such as building jigsaw puzzles and throwing darts (Schleien, Wehman, & Kiernan, 1981). Martin, England, and England (1971), for example, used backward chaining to teach learners with severe disabilities to make their beds. A task analysis was developed and taught in reverse order. The first step taught was the last step of the bed-making task: The learners were presented with a nearly completely made bed and were taught to pull the bedspread over the pillow to complete the task. After mastering this last step, the learners had to complete the final two steps, which were to put the pillow on the bed and then pull the bedspread over the pillow. When these two steps were mastered, the learners had to pull the bedspread back so as to allow room for the pillow, put the pillow on the bed, and then pull the bedspread back over the pillow. The process continued until all 20 steps in the chain had been successfully mastered by the learners.

As another example, Sigafoos (1992) described a backward chaining approach for teaching a 33-year-old woman with developmental disabilities to use a communication wallet. Wallet use was task analyzed into four steps: (1) remove wallet from pocket, (2) open wallet, (3) find the page with the correct symbol on it, and (4) point to the correct symbol. Intervention initially focused on teaching the woman to correctly perform only the fourth step of the request (i.e., pointing to the correct symbol). She was given the wallet, opened to the correct page, and the trainer offered a preferred item and asked, "What do you want?" If the woman pointed to the exposed symbol within 10 seconds, she received a portion of the object. If she did not respond, the trainer modeled the correct response and said, "Do this." Only social praise was given for prompted requests. Next, she was taught the third step, which was to search the pages of the wallet for the correct symbol and then point to it. When this was mastered, she was taught to open the wallet, after which she would reliably complete the third and fourth steps. The first step was then taught to complete the chain.

Although backward chaining has an appealing logic, it also has some potential drawbacks. For example, some research suggests that this procedure may not lead to very strong initial links if the chains contain many separate responses—that is, if the chains are too long. Therefore, trainers need to understand that some learners may not maintain early links if the chain is long and taught using the backward chaining procedure. In such cases, a forward chaining procedure or total task presentation method may be indicated.

Forward Chaining

Forward chaining is almost, but not exactly, the opposite of backward chaining. With forward chaining, the first step in the task is targeted for instruction. When the learner makes the first response, the trainer then completes all of the other steps and gives the learner the reinforcement. Once the learner has mastered the first step, then the second step is added into the training session. Now the learner is expected to independently initiate and complete the first step and then move on to the second step. As always, prompting and fading are used to teach the learner to perform the step, and once the step is mastered, the next step is added and targeted for instruction. Each new step is added one at a time in this forward sequence until the learner performs the whole task.

Consider what happens during a training session after the learner has mastered Steps 1 and 2 but has not been taught Step 3. The session begins, and the learner completes the first step. This produces conditioned reinforcement and creates the discriminative stimulus for initiating the second step, which the learner then completes. Although completion of Step 2 produces the discriminative stimulus for Step 3, it is unlikely that this stimulus will control the learner's behavior at this stage because the required response for completing Step 3 has not yet been taught. Thus, when the discriminative stimulus occurs, the trainer will have to prompt the response and fade the prompts as described in the previous chapters until the learner has acquired Step 3.

During the training on a specific step, when prompts are being faded, the trainer may find it useful to introduce error correction for incorrect responses. It also may facilitate acquisition to use extinction, or the withholding of reinforcement for prompted responses. Although error correction and extinction may facilitate prompt fading when teaching a new link in a behavioral chain, these two strategies may also be aversive to the learner, which could weaken the strength of the chain. One way to assess whether forward chaining weakens stimulus control from one link in a chain to the next would be to determine whether errors are starting to occur on previously mastered steps. For example, error correction and extinction of errors on Step 3 may weaken the chain by inducing errors on Steps 2 and 1. In this situation, one would expect more errors on Step 2 than on Step 1, because links that are closest to the link where error correction and extinction are used are not as strong because they have not been practiced for as long as earlier taught links.

The point is that forward chaining may establish a training situation in which previously trained chains are intermittently reinforced and extinguished if error correction and extinction are used for fading prompts. This situation could weaken the chain and necessitate the continual reestablishment of stimulus control when training is introduced for each new step of the task. Despite this potential problem, forward chaining is used more often than backward chaining, probably because it seems more natural.

Total Task Training

Total task training is perhaps more similar to forward chaining than to backward chaining. Like forward chaining, the total task approach begins with the first step of the task, but training occurs on each and every step of the task during each session until the learner performs the task to the specified performance criterion. As an example, Azrin, Schaeffer, and Wesolowski (1976) used total task training to teach dressing and undressing to learners with developmental disabilities. The total task approach has also been used to teach learners to assemble complex equipment, such as bicycle brakes, carburetors, and lawn mower engines (Gold, 1972; Walls, Ellis, Zane, & Vanderpoel, 1979). Although many of these tasks also have been taught using backward or forward chaining, some tasks appear better suited to a total task approach. A potential advantage of total task training is that differential strengthening of the links in the behavioral chain is less likely than with forward chaining. However, the approach may be more difficult for trainers because they must be prepared to teach every step in the task during every training trial. In addition, the delivery of reinforcement can be difficult. For example, if reinforcement is provided for completing each step, then the learner may receive a considerable amount of reinforcement, which may interfere with the fluency of the task and weaken the power of the final natural reinforcement that arises from completing the task.

Regardless of whether the trainer is intending to use backward chaining, forward chaining, or total task training, it is important to determine whether the learner is able to perform some steps of the task analysis before training starts. If so, there may be no need for separate training on those steps. On the other hand, some instruction may be necessary to make sure that these steps are effectively integrated into the entire behavioral chain, because isolated skills, even if they are already in the learner's repertoire, may not have discriminative and reinforcing functions that are needed for the chain to hang together.

Behavior analysts working in the area of developmental disabilities often recommend backward chaining over the other two approaches. As we mentioned before, backward chaining has the advantage of always having an available conditioned reinforcer to strengthen each new response that is added to the chain. However, this recommendation is based in part on the assumption that completing each step is the only conditioned reinforcer available. Although this may be the case, it is important to note that some learners might already respond to other types of conditioned reinforcers, such as praise, that can be made contingent upon completing each step of the task. Thus, conditioned reinforcement in the form of praise, for example, would seem to be rather easily introduced into the forward and total task approaches, which could make them as effective as backward chaining.

Unfortunately, research focused on examining the relative efficiency of forward, backward, and total task chaining formats is rare and limited to assembly tasks under strictly controlled conditions. One relevant study (McDonnell & McFarland, 1988) compared the forward chaining and total task approaches for teaching learners to wash clothes. The researchers found that the total task approach was associated with faster acquisition and fewer errors.

Many difficulties can arise when attempting to put together a behavioral chain from the sequence of responses taught in a task analysis. For example, although it is not uncommon for one response to actually facilitate the next, it is also possible that one response in the chain may inhibit the next response. For example, communication intervention programs have often focused first on training receptive language skills. For example, the learner is taught to point to objects named by the trainer (e.g., "Point to the ball [cup, spoon, etc.]"). This skill is thought be a prerequisite for learning expressive language (e.g., for the learner to produce the manual sign for ball when shown a ball). However, some studies reveal that the acquisition of a receptive communicative repertoire may in fact inhibit the acquisition of an expressive repertoire (Bucher, 1983; Watters, Wheeler, & Watters, 1981).

Another problem that may arise when an incorrect chaining sequence is used was described by Hoogeveen, Smeets, and Lancioni (1989). These researchers, in the first phase of their study, taught learners with mild to moderate disabilities to read consonant–vowel syllables (e.g., *ni, sa*). In the next phase, the learners were reading vowel–consonant syllables (e.g., *in, as*) as if they were the previously taught consonant–vowel syllables. In this example, the number of errors committed by the learners increased due to incorrect sequencing of response chains and training phases.

ERROR ANALYSIS

Errors made by the learner during training can be a problem for several reasons. Not only can errors slow training and increase the time required to attain criterion, but they also may evoke problem behaviors in the learner and frustrate trainers. It is helpful and at times necessary to undertake an analysis of errors during training.

At least four types of error may occur during training of chained tasks. The first type occurs when the response is not initiated within a predetermined interval following presentation of the stimulus or prompt. This is called a latency or no-response error. The second type, a topographical error, is recorded when the motoric characteristics of the response fail to match the trainer's criterion. For example, the learner might be expected to produce the manual signs "I want more" to request more of an object, but instead the learner produces a different sequence and some irrelevant manual signs (e.g., "You, I, Drink"). The third type, a duration error, is said to occur if the learner fails to complete the behavioral chain within a specific interval of time. The fourth type is a sequence error, which occurs if the learner makes a response out of sequence. For example, when making coffee, the learner might put coffee into the machine before inserting the required coffee filter. Sequence errors account for a large portion of the errors made when teaching a task-analyzed skill, especially if the chain involves many steps. According to Wright and Schuster (1994), up to 50% of the errors made during such training programs are sequence errors.

Given the large percentage of sequence errors, it might be useful to determine whether some sequence errors might be allowed if they do not affect the final outcome. Although one has to put the filter in before the coffee, it does not matter if one fills the coffee maker with water before or after measuring the coffee. Wright and Schuster (1994) compared learner performances on tasks when the order of steps was either prescribed by a task analysis or chosen by the learner. Their results across 4 learners indicated that learner-chosen sequences were acquired in fewer sessions and with fewer errors. The implication of this finding is that chained tasks may be executed with fewer errors if the trainer allows the learner to choose the sequence of steps rather than being taught to follow the steps of some predetermined task analysis. When possible, then, it is appropriate for trainers to allow learners to make such choices. Not only does the learner have more control and input, but learning may be facilitated during multiple-component response training.

SUMMARY AND CONCLUSION

When teaching learners more complicated skills that involve multiple-component responses, the trainer needs to break each skill into teachable steps and then chain those steps together. This chapter has described procedures for conducting a task analysis and for chaining multiple responses together. Responses can be chained together using backward chaining, forward chaining, and total task presentation. There may be advantages to backward chaining, but all three strategies have been used with success when teaching multiple-component responses to learners with developmental disabilities.

Although we have mentioned several times the importance of reinforcement for correct responses, we have not yet provided formal discussion of the concept of reinforcement or of procedures for selecting and delivering reinforcers. This topic is taken up in the next chapter.

Chapter 4

◆◆◆◆◆◆◆◆◆◆◆◆◆◆◆◆◆◆◆◆◆◆◆◆◆◆◆◆◆◆

Preference Assessment and Choice Making

An essential part of one-to-one training is the administration of items that will increase, strengthen, or reinforce the response that has been targeted for instruction. During one-to-one training, a response occurs and a consequence is provided. For example, the learner makes the correct response, and the trainer therefore provides verbal praise plus access to a preferred edible object. The idea is that these types of consequences might be reinforcers for the response. If the consequence that is provided contingent upon a response makes that response more likely to occur on subsequent instructional trials, then the consequence can be defined as a reinforcer.

Suppose an individual makes the manual sign for "water" and then receives a small amount of water to drink. If the manual sign occurs again soon after the person has finished the first drink, one can assume that receipt of the water was probably a reinforcer for the response. As another example, suppose a child is shown a toy and prompted to request it by pointing to a line drawing representing a toy car. After the prompt, the child receives the actual toy car to play with for a few minutes. On the next instructional trial, the child is again shown the toy car and this time points to the correct symbol without being prompted. In this case, receipt of the toy in the first instructional trial was probably a reinforcer because it strengthened the response of pointing to the line drawing. The scenario is shown in Figure 4.1.

Reinforcement of correct responses during training is essential if learning is to occur. In fact, it is not an overstatement to say that the delivery of reinforcement for correct responses is one of the most important aspects of effective training. Many

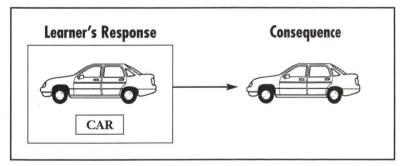

Figure 4.1. Example of a simple reinforcement contingency where the learner points to a drawing and receives access to the corresponding object.

times, the failure of a training program is primarily related to a reinforcement problem of one type or another. Several types of reinforcement problems are common in a floundering training program:

1. Trainers fail to deliver any reinforcing consequences at all.

2. Trainers deliver reinforcement too infrequently to maintain responding.

3. Trainers deliver consequences that they think or hope are reinforcers, when in fact these consequences are not reinforcers for the learner and, therefore, do not strengthen the response.

4. Trainers have reinforcers available to them but fail to deliver these immediately contingent on a correct response. In this case the contingency may be disrupted if too long a delay occurs between the response and the consequence.

5. Trainers deliver consequences for incorrect or no responses, and not only for correct responses.

6. Reinforcers are freely available or provided without the learner's having to first make the desired response.

All of these problems can disrupt the connection between correct responses and reinforcement and, therefore, impair learning.

Other problems can arise from ineffective use of reinforcement, such as from giving too much or too little reinforcement. Furthermore, an item that was reinforcing at the beginning of a training session may lose its reinforcing power after a few trials due to a loss of drive (i.e., satiation). A child who has learned a number of responses to receive food rewards, for example, may show a loss of motivation once she has had enough to eat. In this scenario the child would not be motivated to respond until she becomes hungry again. Learners often fail to make progress during training simply because the items used as consequences are not reinforcers or have temporarily lost whatever reinforcing function they previously had.

Given the importance of reinforcement for learning and the many problems that may arise from ineffective use of reinforcement, it is critical for trainers to identify reinforcers for individual learners. Effectively implementing one-to-one instructional procedures requires the trainer to identify and select consequences that will function as reinforcers during training. One way to do this is to undertake a systematic assessment of the learner's preferences.

Preference assessment refers to a number of strategies, all of which are designed to find out what the learner likes or prefers. The assumption is that items the learner likes or prefers are potential reinforcers. However, this assumption does not always hold because a preferred item may not always function as a reinforcer. For this reason it is helpful to undertake assessments to identify a number of preferred items and to rank order these potential reinforcers from more to less preferred.

A choice-making paradigm (discussed later in this chapter) is often used to rank order preferences. In this paradigm, the learner is presented with repeated opportunities to select an item when given a choice of two or more objects. Items that the learner selects more frequently are presumed to be more preferred than items selected less frequently.

Trainers can identify reinforcers using several procedures that involve preference assessment and choice making. One aim of this chapter is to describe procedures that have been used to identify reinforcers for individuals with developmental disabilities (for additional information, see Lohrmann-O'Rourke & Browder, 1998). After reading this chapter, trainers should be in a better position to select and implement an appropriate procedure for identifying potential reinforcers prior to starting one-to-one training.

Before describing specific preference assessment and choice-making strategies, it is important to point out that for the trainer to implement these procedures, the learner must be capable of performing a number of entry behaviors. Entry behaviors are specific skills that enable the learner to participate in the preference assessment or choice-making task. Although the specific entry behaviors needed for participation vary with the type of procedure used, a number of entry behaviors are common to most types of preference assessment and choice-making tasks. If the learner does not already have these behaviors, then the trainer should conduct an indirect preference assessment. If any of the objects identified in this indirect assessment should prove to be reinforcers, then these could be used during single-component response training to teach the entry behaviors that would allow for a direct assessment of the learner's preferences in the future. Preference assessment is not only an initial step and integral part of all one-to-one training programs, but also a step that should be repeated at regular intervals. Repeated preference assessments are necessary because the learner's preferences are likely to change over time. Conducting preference assessments at regular intervals (e.g., once a month) is one way to increase the probability that the consequences being delivered during training for correct responses are in fact reinforcers.

One important entry behavior is the ability to select or sample the objects or activities that are available. Many learners will come to the task with a fairly obvious and direct way of sampling an object; that is, they will reach out and take an offered item if they want it. The act of reaching out and taking an object could be conceptualized as the learner's way of indicating interest in the object. Drasgow, Halle, Ostrosky, and Harbers (1996) referred to this as behavioral indication. Reaching out and taking an object is usually a clear form of behavioral indication, and the items that the learner most frequently selects typically will be more preferred and more effective reinforcers than items that are rarely or never selected.

However, reaching out for and taking an item is not the only way of indicating one's choices and preferences. Learners with a physical disability, for example, may be incapable of reaching for or grasping an object. In some cases, therefore, it may be necessary to look for other ways, such as eye gaze, facial expressions, and body movements, that a learner might use to indicate choice and preference. Sigafoos (1998) described a number of personal selection strategies that individuals with developmental disabilities might use to indicate preferences and make choices. Table 4.1 lists some of these personal selection strategies.

Another entry behavior is the ability to respond to cues from others to indicate preference or make a choice. For some learners this will be evident by their ability to respond to simple verbal instructions given by a trainer, such as "Take the one you want." In many cases, however, such verbal instructions will be meaningless because the learner has little or no receptive language. In these cases the trainer needs to ensure that the physical arrangement of the task provides an obvious cue for what is expected. For example, two items might be spaced 60 cm apart and placed within easy reach of the learner. The trainer can then look expectantly at the learner or gesture toward the general direction of each item. This arrangement is sufficient to evoke a choice-making response for many learners, even though they fail to respond to the verbal instruction, "Make a choice" (Sigafoos, Laurie, & Pennell, 1995). This choice-making arrangement is shown in Figure 4.2.

Assessment strategies to identify preferences can begin when the learner has a way of sampling objects and indicating a choice, provided that the task can be arranged in such a way as to provide a sufficient cue or discriminative stimulus for evoking a choice-making response. Preference assessment strategies can be classified into two general types: indirect and direct.

TABLE 4.1
Personal Selection Strategies for Indicating
Preferences and Making Choices

Type	Examples
Vocalization	Laugh, cry, groan, hum, sigh
Head nod	Left/right, up/down, roll
Facial expression	Smile, frown, purse lips, grimace
Body movement	Move toward, move away, wiggle
Contact	Reach for item, touch object, tighten grip
Eye gaze	Look at, look away, open/close

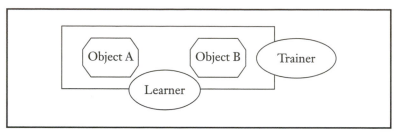

Figure 4.2. Choice-making arrangement.

INDIRECT PREFERENCE ASSESSMENT

Relying on the learner's ability to indicate a preference can be time consuming. It can also be difficult if the learner does not have the required entry behaviors. The trainer may find it beneficial to identify potential reinforcers by conducting an indirect assessment of preferences. An indirect assessment might consist of asking people who know the learner well about the things that the learner seems to like. Significant others can also be interviewed in a more formal way to find out what things the learner apparently prefers. For example, the trainer might ask the caregiver to list three foods, three drinks, three toys, and three leisure activities that the learner likes.

Sigafoos, Didden, and O'Reilly (2003) used an indirect procedure to assess the preferences of children with developmental disabilities. The parents of each child were asked to list food, drink, and toy items that the child liked. From this list, a few items were selected that could be easily delivered as consequences during one-to-one training.

Sigafoos et al. (2003) used this indirect assessment information during one-to-one training. Each of 3 boys with developmental disabilities was taught to request preferred items by pressing a switch on a voice-activated communication aid that triggered the prerecorded message "I want more." Initially, each child was given a small taste of or brief moment with each item (e.g., one potato chip, one sip of juice, and 30 seconds of play with the toys). The trainer then moved the tray of objects out of reach and said, "Let me know if you want more." Typically, at the start of training, the children reached for the tray rather than pressing the switch. However, each child learned the pressing response within 20 minutes of training.

In the Sigafoos et al. (2003) study, the only consequence for a correct switch press during acquisition training was access to the tray of three items, from which the learner could select one item. In this study, it appeared that the indirect assessment of preferences did in fact lead to the identification of effective reinforcers for teaching the requesting response. If any of these 3 children had not shown progress during the training, then one likely explanation might be that access to the objects on the tray was not a reinforcing consequence for pressing the switch. This conclusion would have been more likely had a child not accepted and consumed the food and drinks or played with the toys when given the opportunity. The results of this study indicate that an indirect assessment may be a quick and easy way to identify reinforcers.

An indirect preference assessment, however, may not always lead to reliable and valid information. What a caregiver thinks the individual likes may differ from what the individual would select if a direct assessment of preferences were conducted. In other words, items identified as potential reinforcers through indirect assessment may not necessarily function as actual reinforcers for the particular responses being taught.

Green et al. (1988) demonstrated discrepancies between the results of direct and indirect assessment. They first used a direct strategy to assess the preferences of 7 individuals, ages 12 to 34 years, who had profound mental and physical disabilities. Sessions were conducted in a training room. A trial began when the trainer presented each learner with 1 of 12 items. This is known as the method of successive presentation, which is discussed in the next section of this chapter. If the learner indicated that he or she wanted the item in some way, such as by reaching for and touching the item or by making a positive vocalization, the item was scored as being preferred. An item was recorded as nonpreferred if the learner either avoided or failed to indicate that he or she wanted it, such as by pushing the item away or turning his or her head away. Staff also were asked to rate how much the learner would prefer each item using a 5-point scale (*least preferred* to *most preferred*). A comparison of the results showed that the staff rankings did not correspond very well with the results from the direct assessment. Other studies have reported similar findings, suggesting that indirect reports may fail to identify preferences (Didden, de Moor, Janssen, & Böhm, 2002; Windsor, Piché, & Locke, 1994).

One way to obtain information that is perhaps more reliable is to use a formal structured interview, rather than asking informants to rank order items. One such interview is the Reinforcer Assessment for Individuals with Severe Disabilities (RAISD; Fisher, Piazza, Bowman, & Amari, 1996). During this interview, caregivers are prompted to consider items within several domains, including food, visual, auditory, tactile, and social stimuli. This assessment facilitates the identification of many potential reinforcers and also identifies the conditions under which those potential reinforcers are preferred.

Along these same lines, Matson and colleagues (1999) developed an assessment scale for identifying reinforcers for persons with severe to profound mental retardation. Using the scale, third-party informants have been able to reliably identify various edible and social reinforcers for use in one-to-one training. The scale has good internal consistency and good interrater and test–retest reliability. These psychometric properties suggest that the scale can provide a useful indirect assessment of preferences.

Another assessment tool is the Resident Lifestyle Inventory (RLI), described by Kennedy, Horner, Newton, and Kanda (1990). The inventory lists 144 typical home and community activities that persons with developmental disabilities may prefer. The RLI also might be used as a first (indirect) step in the assessment of preferences. In most cases, however, it will be necessary to undertake a direct assessment of preferences to verify the results of an indirect assessment.

DIRECT PREFERENCE ASSESSMENT

Although a formal interview such as the RAISD or a checklist such as the RLI can facilitate an indirect assessment of preferences, these methods should be considered a first step. Once a list of potential reinforcers has been identified using an indirect assessment, these items can be included in a direct assessment of preferences. Three procedures can be used to conduct a direct assessment of preferences: (a) successive presentation, (b) pairwise presentation or choice making, and (c) simultaneous or the multiple-stimulus mode of presentation. With all three procedures, the items to be presented can be based initially on an indirect assessment. In addition, the trainer should select items for presentation that are easy and safe to present and readily available in the natural environment. Table 4.2 presents a list of items that may be suitable for presenting during a preference assessment for learners with developmental disabilities. Table 4.2 also explains how the item should be presented. For example, to assess whether the learner might like the scent of flowers as a form of olfactory reinforcement, the trainer might present a container of dried hibiscus. If the learner selected the container and smelled its contents each time that it was offered, then the trainer would have some evidence that this form of olfactory stimulation might be useful as a reinforcer for the learner.

As part of the assessment procedure, the trainer needs to develop objective response definitions of the behaviors to be recorded. Useful measures include whether or not the learner points to the item or points to a representation of the item (e.g., a line drawing), vocalizes when shown the item, looks at or moves toward the item, consumes the offered food or drink, and plays with the offered toys (DeLeon & Iwata, 1996; Didden, de Moor, & Bruyns, 1997; Green, Reid, Canipe, & Gardner, 1991; Ivancic & Bailey, 1996; Windsor et al., 1994), or does something else that indicates he or she wants the offered item (e.g., smiles, wiggles excitedly). Measuring the delay between the offer of the item and when the learner makes a selection can also be useful. This measure of response latency may be one way of rank ordering preferences.

Trainers may have difficulty conducting a direct assessment with individuals who do not have a reliable way of making a choice or indicating a preference. For example, individuals with developmental and physical disabilities may have a limited behavioral repertoire or may not be cued by the presentation of offered items to make a choice-making response.

TABLE 4.2

Stimulus Items and Methods of Stimulus Presentation

Stimulus Item	Occasion To Respond
Mirror	Held at a 45° tilt raised toward the child.
Light	Inactive light box placed 20 cm in front of the child.
Song	Inactive tape player placed 20 cm in front of the child.
Beep	Inactive tape player placed 20 cm in front of the child.
Coffee	Closed can with coffee placed 20 cm in front of the child.
Flower	Closed plastic container with hibiscus placed 20 cm in front of the child.
Juice	Cup of juice placed 20 cm in front of the child.
Graham cracker	Piece of cracker placed 20 cm in front of the child.
Vibrator	Inactive vibrator placed 20 cm in front of the child.
Fan	Fan placed down flat 20 cm in front of the child.
Heat pad	Heated cloth placed 20 cm in front of the child.
Cool block	Frozen package placed 20 cm in front of the child.
Swing	Child faced to the swing within reach.
Rock	Therapist's hands placed on the child's chair.
Clap	Therapist brought hands poised to clap within reach of the child.
Hug	Therapist leaned forward with hands outstretched to within 0.5 m of the child.

Note. From "Assessment of Stimulus Preference and Reinforcer Value with Profoundly Retarded Individuals," by G. M. Pace, M. T. Ivancic, G. L. Edwards, B. A. Iwata, and T. J. Page, 1985, *Journal of Applied Behavior Analysis, 18,* 249–255. Copyright 1985 by The Society for the Experimental Analysis of Behavior. Reprinted with permission.

Trainers may need to teach these individuals the response that will enable their participation in a direct assessment of preferences. This could be accomplished using single-component response training as described in Chapters 1 and 2. For example, the learner initially might need to be physically guided to point to an offered item using a most-to-least procedure.

After prompting the response, the trainer gives the learner access to the item, which will hopefully serve as reinforcement for the pointing response. As the prompt is faded, the learner should become independent at making the pointing response.

Successive Presentation

Using the successive presentation method, the trainer presents a single item to the learner for a brief period of time (e.g., 5 seconds) and records the learner's behavior in response to that item. The trainer then presents a second item and records the learner's response. This procedure is repeated for all items. Once each item has been presented a number of times, say 10 to 20 times, the trainer calculates the percentage of times the learner wanted the item. For example, if juice was presented 10 times and the learner reached for and drank the offered juice 9 out of 10 times, then the percentage of acceptance of the juice would be 90%. If, on the other hand, some other item (maybe milk) was presented 10 times but selected only twice (20%), then the trainer could conclude that the learner preferred juice over milk.

The successive presentation method can be useful, but it does have some potential disadvantages. For example, some learners may respond to the presentation of one item not because they want that item, but simply to get it out of the way so as to proceed to the next item. The trainer would then think the first item is preferred when it is not. Generally, the degree of preference for one item may be relative to the degree of preference for the items presented before and after. For example, an item that would ordinarily be neutral, in that the learner would neither approach nor avoid it, may actually become highly preferred if it has been preceded by an item of even lower preference. This means that the rank order of preferences may be influenced by the order of item presentation. The possibility of order effects may explain the discrepancy between direct and indirect assessment results that have often been noted in the literature (Green et al., 1991). One way to minimize order effects would be to present items in a random order. Despite the potential disadvantages, the successive presentation procedure may be a useful strategy, especially when assessing learners who may be unable to make a choice when objects are presented in pairs or simultaneously.

Pairwise Presentation

Pairwise presentation involves a series of paired comparisons in which each item is presented with each of the other items over a number of discrete trials. This procedure is also called the paired-choice or forced-choice method. The choice-making paradigm (discussed in the next section), which usually involves making a choice for one out of two items presented, can be viewed as a special case of the pairwise presentation procedure.

To use this procedure, the trainer might first complete an indirect assessment, using the RAISD, for example. From this the trainer could select the 5 or 10 highest ranking or seemingly most preferred items. These items are then allocated to various pairs (e.g., Item 1 is paired with Item 4, Item 5 with Item 6, Item 9 with Item 3, etc.). The combinations would be randomly determined and counterbalanced across trials. Each item pair is then presented a number of times (e.g., 10 trials), and the percentage of times each item was selected is calculated. For example, if an item was presented 10 times and selected 5 times, the percentage would be 50%. To begin an assessment trial, the trainer presents a pair of items, and the learner is allowed to choose only one of the two items. When presenting each pair, it is important to alter the left–right placement of items across trials to help prevent location-based responding. Because it is also important to pair each item with every other item a number of times (e.g., 10 times) to cover all possible combinations, this approach can become fairly complicated and time consuming.

When conducting a pairwise assessment of preferences, the trainer needs to be consistent in the placement of items. Both items in each pair should always be placed within easy reach of the learner, at an equal distance apart from each other and equally close to the learner. If one item is placed farther away, then the other item might be selected merely because it is closer. The learner must not only be able to see the items in the pair but also be able to easily reach out and take either item or otherwise indicate a choice for one of the two items.

Once the items are placed in front of the learner, the trainer cues the learner that a choice is to be made. This cue is often a verbal instruction (e.g., "Take one" or "Which one do you want?"). For some learners, however, such as those with hearing impairments, the cue might also include a gesture toward the items and an expectant look. These cues are important, especially if the learner has a history of not being allowed to choose desired items. Sometimes, for example, well-meaning caregivers anticipate a learner's wants and needs and eagerly meet these needs without giving the learner an opportunity to make an independent selection. Over time, some of these learners become passive and unlikely to initiate a choice-making response. The trainer must give a cue to indicate that it is now allowable and expected that the learner will take one of the offered items.

Another potential problem during pairwise assessment of preferences is that the learner will attempt to take both items. This problem could arise if the learner prefers both items in the pair, even if not equally. If the learner touches, picks up, or points to two items at the same time, the trainer should gently interrupt the learner's attempt and then repeat the trial by saying something like "Only one" and then moving both items out of reach for 10 seconds. It is not appropriate for the trainer to respond to such attempts by saying "No!" or by removing the items with force. Doing so may make the learner less likely to initiate a choice because of that prior punishment.

When the learner makes a choice, the trainer should provide access to the chosen item. If the learner has chosen a food or beverage, the trainer should provide a small amount of the item and then wait until it has been consumed before offering the next pair of objects. If an activity, such as a toy, book, or cassette tape of music, is selected, then the trainer should allow the learner to access the selected activity for some reasonable duration of time, perhaps 30 to 60 seconds.

On some assessment trials, the learner may not make a choice from the pair of items. If the learner neither approaches nor more directly selects an item within 10 seconds, then the trainer should prompt the learner to sample both items by giving the items to the learner or by engaging in each activity with the learner. The trainer then presents the two items for an additional 10 seconds to determine whether the learner will now show a preference. If the learner still does not make a choice after sampling the items, then a nonselection response is recorded for that trial.

Although a nonselection may indicate that neither item is sufficiently preferred to evoke a response from the learner, in some cases the learner might not make a selection due to lack of familiarity with the items. In such cases, the opportunity to sample each item may provide sufficient experience for the learner to develop a preference. For example, in the study by Didden et al. (2002), an exploration phase preceded the pairwise assessment phase. During the exploration phase, the learner was prompted by the trainer to sample each of six items for 1 minute each.

After sampling, if the learner still does not make a selection within 10 seconds, the trainer removes both items, records that no selection was made for that pair, and initiates the next trial with a different pair of items from the pool. When all pairs of items have been presented a number of times (e.g., 10 times), the trainer can calculate the percentage of times that each item was selected and rank order each item in terms of most to least preferred. The most preferred items (i.e., items selected at least 80% of the time) are more likely to function as reinforcers when training begins to teach specific target responses.

Table 4.3 shows a rank ordering of items based on the percentage of times a young child with autism selected each item during a pairwise assessment of preferences. The data in Table 4.3 suggest that potato chips and the toy truck, and possibly grape juice, would most likely function as effective reinforcers for this child. In contrast, water, yogurt, and the tennis ball were least preferred and would be less effective reinforcers during one-to-one training. The other items (i.e., milk, storybook, and strawberry) may work as backup choices for reinforcers during training.

The data obtained from a pairwise assessment may not always be as nicely ordered as those in Table 4.3. In some cases

TABLE 4.3
Rank Order of Preferences for a Young Child with Autism

Item	% of Time Selected	Rank Order (from most to least preferred)
Potato chip	100	1
Toy truck	80	2
Grape juice	75	3
Strawberry	50	4
Storybook	50	4
Milk	40	5
Tennis ball	20	6
Yogurt	20	6
Water	0	7

an undifferentiated pattern of preferences may emerge. This pattern may indicate that all the items are about equally preferred, which would not necessarily preclude any of the items from serving as reinforcers. However, an undifferentiated pattern also may indicate that none of the items is highly preferred. This would be the case if the learner has to be prompted repeatedly to sample the items. In this situation, all of the items are unlikely to be effective reinforcers. As we mentioned before, one of the reasons why training programs are ineffective is because reinforcers either have not been or cannot be found.

When faced with an undifferentiated pattern, the trainer might obtain greater differentiation by creating more varied pairs of items. Bowman, Piazza, Fisher, Hagopian, and Kogan (1997), for example, found that some learners seemed to prefer a more varied presentation of slightly less preferred items over the constant presentation of items of higher preference. This finding suggests that trainers should take item variation into account when using a pairwise assessment of preferences. For example, if the preferences shown in Table 4.3 showed a less differentiated pattern, then it might be useful for the trainer to

repeat the assessment using a varied combination of less preferred items (e.g., tennis ball + milk, storybook + water).

Choice Making

Several studies have examined choice making in individuals
with developmental disabilities. Because some individuals appear to lack choice-making skills or do not demonstrate them
in natural environments, interventions have been developed
to teach choice-making skills. Sigafoos (1998) emphasized the
importance of increasing skills and opportunities for choice
making. Indeed, the extent to which individuals with developmental disabilities are allowed to make choices is often considered a measure of the quality of services that are provided to
them. To put it strongly, quality of life can be conceptualized
to some extent in terms of the nature of choices available and
the extent to which one is able to exercise choice (Cummins,
1991; Parmenter, 1994).

Unfortunately, individuals with developmental disabilities often lack the skills and the opportunity to make meaningful choices (Stancliffe, 1995). Meaningful choices involve not
only making major life decisions, such as where to live and
work, but also everyday choices, such as what to wear, what to
eat for dinner, and what to listen to on the radio. In addition,
choice making is not confined to making a concrete choice for
one of two items (e.g., coffee vs. tea); it also involves making
more abstract choices, such as when responding to the question
"What do you want?"

For the purpose of assessing preferences, choice making
can be operationalized as selecting from among two or more
available options. In this respect, the use of a choice-making
paradigm for assessing preferences has its limitations. One
limitation might arise if a trainer always uses the learner's most
preferred item as reinforcement for the learner's target behaviors. Over time, the learner might come to respond only to this
consequence. The problem with this scenario is that it may not
always be possible or desirable to allow people to have access to
their most preferred item during instructional sessions. Al-

though a learner might prefer ice cream above all else, it may be a problem to continue to rely on this reinforcer if the person's weight and cholesterol levels start to increase.

The reality is that it is beneficial to ensure that the learner will respond to a number of items that vary in terms of preference. This means that the learner cannot always be given the most preferred item, but instead should be taught to cope with reinforcers having lower preference values. (As an aside, many learners also have to learn to tolerate a delay before reinforcement because it is not always possible or desirable for the trainer to provide immediate reinforcement.)

When a learner's preferences have been assessed using a pairwise presentation method, the learner's ability to make a choice under these assessment conditions may not occur in more natural settings, such as when the individual is offered tea or coffee for break time in a vocational setting (Vaughn & Horner, 1995). This lack of generalization is a common problem in training programs for individuals with developmental disabilities (see Chapter 6). One way to overcome this generalization problem and create opportunities for choice making is for the trainer or others to provide in the natural setting the same pairwise presentation format used to assess preferences. For example, direct-care staff might offer two different beverages at break time and ask the person, "Which one do you want? Coffee or tea?" Although teaching consistent choice-making skills may require a relatively extensive training program, its benefits seem clear. Not only can enhancement of choice making lead to improved quality of life, but the development of choice-making skills may result in increased participation in functional activities (Mithaug & Hanawalt, 1978; Mithaug & Mar, 1980) and decreases in problem behaviors (Dunlap et al., 1994).

Although evidence suggests that even individuals with the most profound disabilities are capable of making choices (Sigafoos et al., 1995), the validity of the choices made is sometimes difficult to determine. That is, it may be unclear if the choices some learners make are true indications of their preferences. The chosen items may not in fact be preferred and might even be nonpreferred or aversive.

The question of validity of choice making was addressed by Sigafoos and Dempsey (1992). This study involved 3 children with multiple disabilities. Each learner appeared to use various idiosyncratic gestures (i.e., looking at items, moving toward items) that appeared to function as choice-making behaviors. Because it was unclear whether these gestures were true indicators of the children's choices and preferences, a validity assessment was conducted in the children's classroom during snack time. Each learner was given the opportunity to choose between food and beverage items. For each assessment trial, the teacher placed small portions of two items in front of the child. A choice was recorded when the learner directed one of the previously defined idiosyncratic gestures to one of the items within 15 seconds. After a choice had been made, the teacher placed the chosen item in the child's hand and physically guided him or her to bring the item to the mouth. The teacher also watched for an indication of acceptance or refusal of the item.

The validity assessment involved two conditions. During the first condition, when the learner indicated a choice for one item, that same item was presented to the learner to accept or refuse. In the second condition, however, the learner was given the nonchosen item. Percentages of acceptance (i.e., consuming the item) and refusal (i.e., dropping the item, turning head away, expelling the item) during the two conditions were compared. The results showed that each learner consistently chose one of the two offered items. Furthermore, all learners showed higher percentages of refusal when they were given the nonchosen item than when given the chosen item. These results suggested that idiosyncratic gestures functioned as valid choice-making behaviors.

In a related study, Duker, Dortmans, and Lodder (1993) taught 5 learners who had severe and profound developmental disabilities to request preferred objects by using communicative gestures. Sometimes after a learner had made a request, he or she was given an item different from the one requested. For example, after requesting a puzzle, the learner was given a sip of juice instead. Duker et al. found that these learners often accepted the wrong item, which might be viewed as a type of error or invalid request. This is a problem because if the learner accepts an item that does not match his or her request, it makes the requesting repertoire less functional. Duker et al. went on to show that a correction procedure could be used to teach the learners to reject the wrong item by repeating the original sign. During correction training, the trainer physically prevented the learner from accepting the wrong item and also physically prompted the learner to repeat the original request. This repetition of the original request could be viewed as a type of repair strategy to be used by the learner when his or her initial request does not result in the appropriate consequence (Brady & Halle, 2002).

Simultaneous Presentation

Another direct method for assessing preferences involves the simultaneous presentation of multiple items. On each assessment trial, the learner might be presented with an array of 10 items and allowed to select one. After each selection, the array is replenished and the same 10 items are presented. This process might be repeated 20 to 30 times to identify those items that are most frequently selected. This is also known as the multiple-stimulus method. One potential advantage of this procedure is that it may provide a quick way of assessing preferences. A disadvantage is that the same items are available on every trial, so the learner may repeatedly choose only one or a few items. Although this technique would provide information about the learner's most highly preferred item or items, it might not enable the trainer to develop a rank order of items in terms of preference. As a result the trainer might be led to use only the most highly preferred items during intervention, which can be a problem for the reasons already mentioned in the previous section.

To ameliorate this potential problem, DeLeon and Iwata (1996) modified the simultaneous presentation method in such a way that it retained its efficiency but prevented the learner from always choosing the same item more than once. What they did was simply not replace items once they had been selected. During the first assessment trial, seven items were in the array that was offered to the learner. The learner could select any one of the seven items. On the next trial, however, only the six remaining items were offered. Then only the five remaining items were offered, and so forth. This procedure, called the multiple-stimulus method without replacement, has proven to be a more efficient way of assessing preferences than the pairwise presentation method. Because of its efficiency, this procedure can be used preceding each training session to assess whether a learner's preferences have changed since the last session. Preference assessment should be seen as an ongoing process.

Ortiz and Carr (2000) described another modification of the simultaneous format. They presented an array of numerous items to learners, who were allowed to interact with any of the items at any time. With this procedure, preference was quantified in terms of the amount of time the learner interacted with each item. This rather novel procedure appears to be useful and efficient, but more research is needed to identify the optimal number of items and the optimal length of assessment. It is unclear, for example, whether presentation of 20 items as compared to, say, 5 items might cause any problems that would invalidate the results of this procedure. It is conceivable that presenting too many items simultaneously might evoke behaviors that differ from the behaviors evoked by presenting only one or two items.

COMPARATIVE STUDIES

In determining which method to use to assess preferences, the trainer should consider four criteria: (a) the extent to which the procedure enables one to rank order items in terms of preferences (i.e., differentiation of preference), (b) the stability of the learner's preferences over time, (c) the ease or efficiency of the procedure, and (d) the extent to which the method leads to a reliable and valid assessment of preferences. Although the best method may depend on the learner, some studies have attempted to compare various preference assessment methods.

Successive Versus Pairwise

Fisher et al. (1992) compared the successive presentation and the pairwise formats. The study involved 4 learners with severe and multiple disabilities, who ranged from 2 to 10 years of age. During the successive format, 16 items were presented one at a time while the researchers recorded the learners' approach and nonapproach behaviors. During the pairwise format, the same 16 stimuli were presented in pairs for a total of 120 trials. Results show that all of the items identified as highly preferred (i.e., chosen in at least 80% of the trials) by the pairwise format were also identified as highly preferred by the successive format. The fact that the two procedures yielded similar results provided a form of interassessment reliability or concurrent validity. On the other hand, some discrepancies appeared in the results across the two procedures: Some items identified as highly preferred in the successive format were only moderately preferred in the pairwise approach. Fisher et al. concluded that the pairwise presentation format results in a stronger differentiation of preferences than the successive presentation format. Nevertheless, the authors stated that the successive presentation format may be better suited to individuals who lack the choice-making skills necessary to participate in a pairwise assessment of preferences.

In another relevant study, Paclawskyj and Vollmer (1995) compared pairwise and successive presentation methods in a study of 4 learners, 8 to 13 years of age, with developmental disabilities and visual impairments. Because of their visual impairments, the assessment methods had to be modified by initially physically guiding the learners to explore each available item. During an assessment trial using the successive presentation method, the trainer physically guided the learner to initially explore each item by touching it for 3 seconds and then to withdraw his or her hand(s) from the object. The trainer then recorded whether the learner approached (i.e., reached for) or avoided the item. For trials involving the pairwise format, the trainer initially guided the learner to explore each item by first touching the left item, then touching the right item, for 3 seconds each. After this exploration, the learner was guided to withdraw his or her hands from the objects. The trainer then recorded which, if either, of the two items the learner reached for. The results from this study indicated that the pairwise format produced a greater differentiation of preferences in terms of rank ordering than did the successive format for all 4 learners. Paclawskyj and Vollmer concluded that the pairwise format appears to be the more effective and reliable method for identifying preference hierarchies in individuals with intellectual and visual impairments.

Simultaneous Versus Pairwise

Windsor et al. (1994) compared the preference rankings obtained with the simultaneous versus the pairwise format with 8 adults who had severe to profound developmental disabilities. Six small portions of food and drink items were used. With the simultaneous format, all six items were presented to the learner at the same time across each of 10 trials. The position of the items was randomly changed after each trial, and each item appeared at least once but no more than twice in each location. With the pairwise format, each item was paired with every other item five times for a total of 30 trials. For each trial, the trainer asked the learner, "Which one do you want?" and then recorded which, if either, item was selected. A selection was recorded if the learner touched an item within 20 seconds. If the learner touched more than one item, the first one touched was recorded as having been selected. A nonselection was recorded if the learner did not touch an item within 20 seconds.

To assess the stability of preferences, 10 such sessions were conducted over a 2-month period. The simultaneous and pairwise rankings were consistent for 5 of the 8 learners. Also, the identical item was identified as most preferred in the two formats by 6 of the learners. Windsor et al. (1994) also assessed the extent to which rankings of preferences were stable across time for the two formats. The mean correlations across presentations were .49 and .63 for the simultaneous format and the pairwise format, respectively. All of the correlations for the pairwise presentation were statistically significant, and five of the eight correlations for the simultaneous format were statistically significant. These data suggest that the pairwise format tended to produce a more consistent ranking of preferences across sessions than the simultaneous format. An important finding from a practical perspective was that the time required to complete the simultaneous format ranged from 3 to 10 minutes, whereas the time needed to complete the pairwise format ranged from 10 to 22 minutes, rendering the former more efficient in terms of session duration.

VALIDATION OF PREFERENCE ASSESSMENT

Some of the main reasons for conducting a preference assessment are (a) to identify items that the learner prefers, as these may function as reinforcers during one-to-one training, and (b) to provide a rank order of items in terms of degree of preferences. In other words, the goal is to find out what the learner likes and how much he or she likes each item. The learner's quality of life can then be improved through increased access to preferred items. In addition, quality of life can be improved by learning new skills, and for this to occur, effective reinforcers are needed. Preferred items are likely to function as effective reinforcers during training programs to teach new skills.

Whether or not an item will function as a reinforcer can never be determined, however, on the basis of preference assessment alone. A reinforcer is something that functions to increase the frequency or duration of a response. Reinforcement refers to the effect of a consequence on a response. If the presentation of a preferred item, contingent upon a response, functions to increase the probability of that response, then it is proper to speak of the preferred item as a reinforcer. If the presentation of a preferred item, contingent upon a response, does not increase the future probability of that response, then the preferred item is not a reinforcer. It is necessary to evaluate whether preferred items are in fact reinforcers for target behaviors. This process of evaluation is referred to as the validation of preference assessment.

Pace, Ivancic, Edwards, Iwata, and Page (1985), in a study using a successive presentation format, defined preferred items as those the learner approached during at least 80% of the trials, and nonpreferred items as those approached in 50% or less of the trials. In their second study, Pace et al. assessed the reinforcing value of preferred and nonpreferred items. The target behaviors were motor responses to verbal instructions, such as "reach," "look," "raise your hand," "touch my hand," and "say 'eat.'" During a preferred condition, a preferred item was delivered contingent upon a correct target response, whereas in the nonpreferred condition, a nonpreferred item was used instead. The results showed that preferred items increased the rate of the target responses more than nonpreferred items did. These data thus provide some validation of the successive presentation procedure. Items identified as preferred in the successive method were reinforcers, whereas items identified as nonpreferred were not reinforcers.

Piazza, Fisher, Hagopian, Bowman, and Toole (1996) also addressed the question of validity of preference assessment. They assessed whether items that had been identified as high, middle, and low in terms of preference would differ in terms of their reinforcing effectiveness. The study involved 4 males with profound developmental disabilities, who ranged from 7 to 19 years of age. Prior to undertaking the direct assessment of preferences, researchers used indirect methods to identify 16 items for each learner that direct-care staff thought might be potential reinforcers. Next, for pairwise assessment, each item was paired once with every other item, and the learner was allowed to choose between the two. Based on the choices made, items were then assigned to one of three categories depending on the percentage of trials on which each item had been chosen. The three categories were high, middle, or low preference. Highly preferred items were defined as the three items most often chosen. Middle items were those chosen closest to the median percentage of trials, or more precisely, the 7th, 8th, and 9th ranked items. Low-preference items were the three chosen least often. The authors hypothesized that an item belonging to the highly preferred category would result in a stronger increase in responding during training when compared to items in the other two categories.

Following the pairwise assessment of preferences, one target behavior was selected for each learner. Target responses were staying either in seat or in a particular location in the room. Because these target behaviors were already in each learner's repertoire, a lack of change in frequency could not be attributed to a skill deficit. Training sessions lasted 10 minutes and involved giving either a high-, middle-, or low-preference item or giving no item (i.e., no reinforcement) contingent upon the target behavior. The duration of target behaviors was recorded, and the results showed that items identified as highly preferred functioned as more effective reinforcers when compared to middle- and low-preference items. In fact, items identified as low preference failed to function as reinforcers for any learner. Thus, the pairwise item assessment procedure appeared to be a valid predictor of reinforcer efficacy.

SUMMARY AND CONCLUSION

Although the pairwise presentation method appears to be a reliable and valid way to identify preferences, it may not be a viable procedure for learners with limited choice-making skills. In such cases, the successive presentation format may be a better method to assess preferences, and the trainer may have to look for subtle approach and avoidance responses because, in the absence of conventional choice-making skills, these may represent the learner's personal selection strategy and indeed his or her only way of indicating a preference. Subtle behaviors might include merely smiling at or looking toward an object, or some other facial expression that occurs when an object is offered. The latency of response may also be an indicator of preference. Ivancic and Bailey (1996), for example, found that differences in the latency of responding were related to differential preferences for items.

Although the successive format can be used with learners who lack more conventional choice-making skills, it is important to note that this procedure might produce false positives—that is, items identified as preferred that do not in fact function as reinforcers (Paclawskyj & Vollmer, 1995). For example, the learner might look at an item not because he or she likes it but, rather, because of a tendency to orient toward presented objects or perhaps because the learner is trying to figure out what it is. On the other hand, the simultaneous presentation format may produce what are called false negatives—that is, items identified as nonpreferred that in fact are preferred and do function as reinforcers. This can occur if the learner always chooses the same item because it is the most preferred, but would also choose some of the other items if they were presented alone. These other items may in fact be only slightly less preferred than the most preferred item. For example, a learner might always choose juice, but would readily accept water if juice was not available. Such false negatives were tested by DeLeon and Iwata (1996), who found that items considered nonpreferred in a simultaneous format, based on an 80% criterion, were nonetheless effective in increasing responding. A similar point was made by Ortiz and Carr (2000) related to their use of the open-ended assessment in which all items were presented and the learner was permitted to move among items over a period of time. This method also seemed to lead to many false negatives, because the learner might not have the time to interact with each item.

These results bring up the issue of whether the 80% rule is a good one. Researchers often employ a cutoff score of 80% to distinguish between preferred and nonpreferred items during preference assessments. Items are identified as preferred if they are chosen in at least 80% of the assessment trials. Although learners may show differential preferences across items, perhaps only one item is chosen on at least 80% of the trials. Then, if a relatively large number of trials is required during training, the use of only one item, even if it is highly preferred, could be a problem because the learner may become satiated with the item and lose interest in the learning activity. It would be better to have a number of preferred items available as reinforcers during training rather than relying on one highly preferred item. Variety is the spice of life. Egel (1981), for example, demonstrated the importance of reinforcer variation in teaching autistic children. Varied reinforcement was better than a single constant reinforcer. We suggest using at least three or four preferred items, even if some of these items do not pass the 80% criterion during preference assessment. Fisher et al. (1996) provided evidence that supports this suggestion.

Another issue arises from the fact that preferences may not be stable. Preference hierarchies tend to change across time. An item that was highly preferred one day or one week may be only moderately preferred the next day or the next week (Houlihan, Jones, & Sloane, 1992; Windsor et al., 1994). As we have previously stated, preference assessments should be repeated regularly to ensure that items being used as reinforcers represent the most up-to-date preferences.

Although indirect methods of preference assessment—that is, parent, staff, and teacher reports and checklists—remain the methods most often used, they should be used with caution because they may not be reliable and valid. Information gained from an indirect assessment should be verified through a more direct assessment of preferences.

Chapter 5

◆◆◆◆◆◆◆◆◆◆◆◆◆◆◆◆◆◆◆◆◆◆◆◆◆◆◆◆◆◆

Managing Problem
Behavior During Training

Some learners may engage in problem behaviors during one-to-one training. Common forms of problem behavior among individuals with developmental disabilities include aggression, self-injury, property destruction, tantrums, and stereotyped movements (Luiselli & Cameron, 1998). The trainer can safely ignore many low-level or infrequent problem behaviors and continue the training without alteration. However, the trainer cannot ignore problem behaviors that are frequent or severe, especially if they might cause injury and damage or seriously disrupt teaching efforts and hinder learning. Because the learner with serious problem behaviors is at greater risk of being excluded from educational activities (Carr, Taylor, & Robinson, 1991), the trainer needs to learn to manage problem behaviors.

The response of trainers to problem behaviors that occur during one-to-one training is a very important part of the instructional program. Part of learning how to be a good trainer is learning how to respond to problem behaviors that occur during training. The first rule of thumb is that the training session should not be stopped in response to problem behavior. Instead, the trainer needs to incorporate effective behavior management strategies into the session so that problem behaviors are not reinforced. The aim of this chapter is to describe behavior management strategies that can be incorporated into one-to-one training so as to reduce problem behaviors.

UNDERSTANDING THE FUNCTION OR PURPOSE OF PROBLEM BEHAVIOR

It is important for trainers to understand the reasons why problem behaviors may occur during one-to-one training. Studies (e.g., Iwata et al., 1994) have shown that these behaviors often serve a function or purpose for the individual. Knowing the function or purpose can guide trainers in selecting effective procedures to manage problem behaviors during one-to-one training. Evidence suggests that there are three major reasons why problem behaviors occur (Iwata et al., 1994): (a) as a way of escaping from or avoiding nonpreferred objects or activities; (b) as a way of gaining access to preferred objects or activities, such as gaining the trainer's attention or access to a preferred toy; and (c) because the very act of engaging in the behavior provides the learner with some type of preferred sensory stimulation. For example, the learner may rock back and forth because this produces a pleasant vestibular sensation. Although problem behavior may occur for other reasons (e.g., physical discomfort), these three factors seem to account for a large percentage of the problem behaviors that a trainer faces when implementing one-to-one training with learners who have developmental disabilities. In the following paragraphs, we consider each of the major functions in more detail.

Escape-Motivated Problem Behavior

Evidence suggests that the requirement to participate in one-to-one training may set the occasion for problem behavior, at least in some learners (Carr & Newsom, 1985). In some cases, then, participation in one-to-one training might be viewed as a task that the learner may not initially enjoy and, therefore, might try to escape or avoid by engaging in problem behavior. In such cases, if the trainer stops the task and withdraws the task demands in response to the learner's problem behavior, this may in fact reinforce and strengthen the problem behavior. Problem behaviors that occur for this reason are known as escape-motivated problem behaviors because their motivation is the escape from or avoidance of a nonpreferred task. In summary, some problem behaviors may occur because in the past they have enabled the learner to escape from or avoid the task. Escape from the task can be viewed as a form of (negative) reinforcement.

Attention-Motivated and Object-Motivated Problem Behavior

In other cases, problem behavior might occur because in the past the behavior has been followed by access to a preferred object or activity, such as attention from others or access to a preferred toy. If the consequences are reinforcers for the learner's problem behavior, then even the occasional receipt of such consequences may be sufficient to maintain problem behavior during training. In this case, the receipt of attention or the toy, for example, can be viewed as a form of positive reinforcement. Trainers, therefore, should be careful not to provide attention or access to preferred items in response to problem behavior. Although giving the learner attention or access to some preferred item may in fact stop the behavior temporarily, it will make the behavior worse in the long run. Even a verbal reprimand (e.g., "Stop that") that is intended to stop the problem behavior involves giving attention, and therefore may function as a form of positive social reinforcement for some learners. Evidence shows that attention and access to preferred objects are often the reinforcers that maintain problem behavior in learners with developmental disabilities (Iwata et al., 1994).

Sensory-Motivated Problem Behavior

Some learners may engage in problem behaviors because the act itself is reinforcing. In such cases it is said that the behavior is automatically reinforced (Iwata et al., 1994). The behavior itself may have direct consequences, which feel good, taste good, or smell good to the learner. A learner might flap his or her hands or rock back and forth in the chair during training because it provides sensory stimulation (Lovaas, Newsom, & Hickman, 1987). In a study involving one-to-one instruction to teach communicative requesting, Roberts-Pennell and Sigafoos (1999) observed that stereotyped behavior in one boy with severe autism occurred most consistently during intertrial intervals, that is, during the few seconds that elapsed from one trial to the next. The trainer had to interrupt the stereotyped movements to get the child back on task, and doing this often led to the boy's slapping his own face. The point is that the pacing of instructional trials may be an important variable related to the occurrence of problem behavior during one-to-one training.

FUNCTIONAL ANALYSIS OF PROBLEM BEHAVIOR

It is often difficult to determine whether problem behavior is related to reinforcement that is negative (i.e., escape, avoidance), positive (e.g., attention, tangibles), or automatic (e.g., sensory stimulation) simply from the form or topography of the behavior. To identify the function or purpose of problem behavior, the trainer needs to isolate the antecedents that set the occasion for the behavior and identify the consequences that maintain the behavior. Behavior that looks as if it were a way of gaining attention may in fact be a way of escaping from a task. For example, one 4-year-old boy with autism regularly got out of his chair during one-to-one training to approach the trainer and give her a hug. At first, the trainer was pleased with his spontaneous displays of affection, but as they became more frequent, she realized that he was seeking attention as a way of escaping the task. Similarly, another child continually ran off during training to a shelf full of toys. The trainer thought he wanted a toy, but it turned out that he only wanted toys when he was expected to work on a task. The behavior of running to the toys was more likely another way of escaping from the task. Another example is stereotyped movements. Although these sometimes are maintained by automatic reinforcement, some learners engage in stereotyped movements during training because then the trainer gives up and stops the task. Durand and Carr (1987), for example, found that for 4 learners with autism, the rate of stereotypic body rocking and hand flapping was related to task difficulty, suggesting that these problem behaviors were in fact escape motivated.

From our experience it appears that most problem behaviors that occur during training are related to escape and avoidance. Therefore, this chapter focuses mainly on procedures to reduce escape-motivated problem behaviors that occur during one-to-one training. Because the learner generally receives frequent attention from the trainer during one-to-one training, the learner should have little motivation to engage in problem behavior related to gaining attention. Other problem behaviors are related to gaining access to the preferred items that are used as reinforcers during one-to-one training. A learner, for example, might begin a session by reaching repeatedly for the reinforcers. If the trainer blocks this attempt to grab one of the reinforcers, then the learner might escalate to problem behavior (e.g., screaming, hitting, head-banging). Such object-motivated behavior problems usually disappear quickly once the learner has completed a few instructional trials and has received several reinforcements. If reaching and grabbing and escalation to problem behaviors persist, however, then the learner is likely not experiencing enough success during training. In this case the trainer should return to a previous and easier step in the training sequence or use more effective prompting strategies to ensure that most training trials end with a correct response, which can then be reinforced.

When problem behaviors persist during training even when the learner receives frequent attention from the trainer and is receiving a high rate of reinforcement for correct responses, the problem behaviors are likely escape motivated. In such a case, it is useful to determine whether the presentation of the task demands reliably evokes the problem behavior and whether withdrawal of task demands is associated with an abrupt cessation of the problem behavior. When the effects of this manipulation (i.e., presentation and withdrawal of task demands) are examined systematically, the resulting data can be used to either confirm or refute a trainer's preliminary hypothesis as to the function or purpose of the problem behavior.

The data shown in Figure 5.1 were collected in the classroom of a 9-year-old boy (Patrick) with profound developmental disabilities and cerebral palsy. Because one of the educational goals was to improve Patrick's mobility, every day the teacher would bring out a walking frame and try to teach Patrick to use the device to walk across the room. The instructional procedure involved most-to-least prompting. However, as shown by the black squares on the graph, representing the demand condition, whenever he was required to use the device to practice walking, Patrick would tantrum at high rates regardless of whether he was prompted to walk 20 meters, 12 meters, or even 3 meters. Indeed, often the mere sight of the walking frame was enough to start a tantrum. In contrast, the figure also shows that tantrums were less likely to occur when the task demands were withdrawn, as indicated by the light-colored

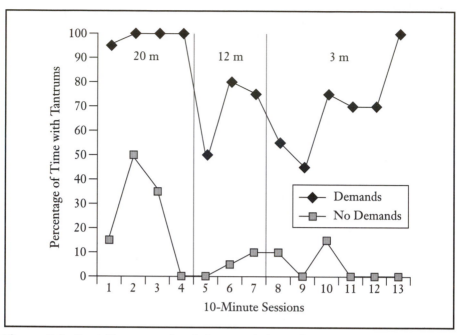

Figure 5.1. Patrick's tantrums in relation to task demands. *Note.* m = meters.

squares. Once the task ended, Patrick's tantrums tended to deescalate quite rapidly. He might cry and thrash about for 30 to 60 seconds, but would then calm down. Based on this assessment, the teacher concluded that Patrick's tantrums were in fact escape motivated.

In this case, the task was important to ensure that Patrick received daily exercise and walking practice, as he was otherwise wheelchair bound. The teacher needed to find a way to reduce his tantrums and increase his participation in the task so as to achieve the therapeutic goals. To make sure that Patrick completed the task of walking across the room, no matter how much he cried, screamed, and thrashed about, the teacher implemented an escape extinction procedure. During the procedure the teacher was careful to make sure that Patrick did not injure himself, and when his tantrums stopped, he received verbal praise and tangible reinforcement. In addition, the task stopped only when he was no longer having a tantrum. With this procedure, tantrums stopped after only five sessions. Then the teacher expanded the walking program, and Patrick learned to become more independent and to take longer walks. Eventually, Patrick seemed to enjoy the activity and was exposed to many new sources of stimulation as he walked around the school as part of his instructional program.

The assessment undertaken with Patrick, as shown in Figure 5.1, might be viewed as a form of hypothesis testing. The teacher had a hypothesis as to why Patrick was engaging in tantrums and designed an assessment to verify the hypothesis. In cases without an initial hypothesis, however, the trainer may need to undertake a more complete functional analysis using analog methodology (Sturmey, 1995). During an analog assessment, the rate of problem behavior is recorded during 10-minute sessions and under various conditions. The conditions differ in terms of antecedents presented to the learner and consequences that are arranged for problem behavior. The various conditions are designed to assess whether the behavior is controlled by positive, negative, or automatic reinforcement. Each condition is usually presented in successive sessions, and this procedure may continue for 5 to 7 days or until trends appear in the data. Analog assessments are labor and resource intensive and require a trainer who has considerable expertise and experience.

To reduce the effort involved in undertaking an analog assessment, some researchers have developed and validated briefer procedures. For example, Derby et al. (1992) used a brief assessment with 79 clients who displayed a variety of problem behaviors. One 10-minute session was conducted under each of the test conditions. They found that in 24 (or 30%) of the cases, problem behavior occurred most frequently under the task demand condition, suggesting that the behaviors were escape motivated. These data are consistent with those of Iwata et al. (1994), who found that self-injurious behavior was often (38%) maintained by negative reinforcement. These various data confirm that the problem behaviors that occur during one-to-one training are often escape motivated.

Researchers have tried to isolate the antecedent conditions and consequences that influence escape-motivated problem behaviors during instructional programs. Carr, Newsom, and Binkoff (1976), for example, recorded the rate of self-injurious behavior in an 8-year-old boy with mild developmental disabilities. His self-injury was recorded under three conditions. In the first condition, the child and a trainer were present in a training room and no demands were placed on the child. The second condition was identical to the first, except that the trainer made a comment to the child every 30 seconds (e.g., "The birds are singing"). The third (i.e., demand) condition was designed to approximate a classroom-learning task. During the demand condition, the trainer presented a series of 20 instructions to the child (e.g., "Point to the window"). If the child did not respond to the instruction, the trainer looked away from him. Self-injurious behavior occurred at a high rate during the demand condition and was virtually absent during the other two conditions. Furthermore, during the demand condition, the child showed several other problem behaviors, such as crying and yelling, that were absent during the other two conditions. Based on this evidence, the researchers concluded that the presentation of an instructional task was the discriminative stimulus for the child to exhibit self-injurious and related problem behaviors and that these problem behaviors were probably, therefore, escape motivated.

The Carr et al. (1976) study was replicated and extended by Gaylord-Ross, Weeks, and Lipner in 1980. This study involved a 16-year-old girl with developmental disabilities who showed severe self-injury. The rates of her self-injury and other problem behaviors were assessed during two task conditions and one nontask condition. During the first task condition, the girl was verbally and physically prompted to complete a jigsaw puzzle. During the second task condition, she was prompted to complete a match-to-sample task. During the nontask condition, no demands were placed on her, although task materials were present. During the initial assessment phase, the rate of verbal and physical prompting was kept constant at one per minute. During the next phase, instructional prompts were given every 30 or 60 seconds. Instances of self-injury occurred most often during the matching task (54%) but only 16% of the time during the jigsaw task and almost never during the nontask condition. In addition, there was a relationship between self-injury and the rate of the trainer's instructions. The 30-second schedule of instructional directives was associated with more frequent self-injury than the 60-second schedule of giving instructions. These results demonstrate that escape-motivated problem behavior can be differentially related to the type of task (i.e., a preference for one task over the other) or to the rate or pace of instructional demands.

In addition to preference and rate of demands, Carr and Durand (1985) found that escape-maintained problem behaviors can also vary with task difficulty. In this study the learners were 4 children with severe developmental disabilities who showed a variety of problem behaviors. Sessions were conducted in a small room in which the trainer and 2 children were present. In a given session, a child received either an easy task or a difficult task. The easy task involved receptive labeling and match-to-sample activities that the learners had mastered correctly 100% of the time. The difficult task, in contrast, was configured so that children were correct only 50% of the time. In addition to manipulating the level of task difficulty, Carr and Durand also manipulated the amount of trainer attention; that is, across sessions the amount of attention from the trainer varied from low (33% of trials) to high (100% of trials). The authors found that problem behavior was completely absent during sessions in which the task was easy and the amount of trainer attention was high. However, 2 of the 4 learners showed high rates of problem behaviors when the task was difficult, suggesting that their behaviors were escape motivated. The third learner showed more problem behavior during the low-attention condition, suggesting that the behavior was attention maintained. The rate of problem behavior for the fourth learner was high when the task was difficult and attention was low, suggesting that the behavior was both escape motivated and attention motivated.

When escape-motivated problem behaviors occur during a task, any stimulus that is temporarily or functionally related to the termination of the task (perhaps something such as the trainer saying "Last one" or "One more minute," or even the act of the trainer starting to pack away the materials) may become a so-called safety signal for the learner. A safety signal is a cue to the learner that the task is about to end. Safety signals acquire their discriminative stimulus properties due to the temporal association between the stimulus and the end of the task.

Carr, Newsom, and Binkoff (1980) demonstrated the effects of a safety signal on the rate of escape-motivated aggressive behavior during instructional tasks with 2 learners with developmental disabilities. The rate of aggressive behavior was assessed during two conditions: demand and no demand. The results showed that both learners had high rates of aggressive behavior during the demand condition, but no aggression when demands were absent. These data suggest that their aggressive behaviors were probably escape motivated and related to task demands. Carr et al. (1980) then investigated the effects of imposing a safety signal onto the demand condition. In one condition, the trainer presented the safety signal after the learners had been working on the task for 5 minutes. After the trainer presented the safety signal, no further demands were placed on the learners for the remainder of the session. A second condition was similar except that the trainer did not present the safety signal. Carr et al. found a high rate of aggressive behaviors during the first half of the safety signal condition, but aggression stopped once the safety signal had been presented. In contrast, the rate of aggression showed no decrease during the second half of the non–safety signal condition, despite the fact that after 5 minutes of this session no more demands were made of the learners. This result suggests that the learners associated the safety signal with withdrawal of task demands. A trainer, therefore, might introduce the safety signal earlier and earlier as a way of reducing problem behaviors that occur during the early portion of a task; however, the effectiveness may depend on the duration of the task and the amount of time that elapses from the onset of the safety signal to the termination of the task.

Along these lines, Smith, Iwata, Goh, and Shore (1995) investigated the effect of training session duration, in terms of number of trials, on the frequency of escape-motivated problem behavior. The study involved 5 learners with developmental disabilities. During each 15-minute session, the learners were asked to complete a simple task. One instructional prompt was given every 30 seconds. If the learner did not perform the response, then the trainer would prompt the response using a most-to-least procedure. If problem behavior (i.e., self-injury) occurred, the trial was terminated. The data revealed three patterns of responding across the 5 learners. For 2 learners, the frequency of self-injury increased during the second half of the session, but with 2 other learners, self-injury decreased as the session progressed. No clear trend was obtained with the fifth learner. These data suggest that problem behavior may have a specific within-session pattern, although the nature of this pattern is likely to vary from one learner to the other. The pattern that a learner shows during a session may have implications for when the trainer should introduce a safety signal, but there is as yet no evidence as to whether or how such patterns may interact with the use of a safety signal procedure.

Apart from the task itself, some learners may try to escape from the social interaction that occurs during training. Some children with autism, for example, do not seem to enjoy social interaction and attempt to escape from or avoid interaction with other people. The avoidance response may include problem behavior, such as hitting that person in an attempt to get that person to go away. In such cases, it might be said that the behavior is a form of social avoidance. During one-to-one training, it may be difficult to determine whether problem behavior is related to task avoidance or to social avoidance. Knowing the difference is critical because different behavior management procedures are indicated for these two functions.

Taylor, Ekdahl, Romanczyk, and Miller (1994) developed a procedure to differentiate task avoidance from social avoidance behavior during a training program. They organized two groups of learners who had autism and related developmental disabilities and who engaged in problem behaviors that appeared to be related to task avoidance or social avoidance. They found that the problem behavior of 2 learners, which appeared to serve a social avoidance function, was higher during an assessment condition when the trainer made requests and social statements than when the trainer ignored the learner. This result provided some confirmation that the problem behaviors of these 2 learners were related to social avoidance. With 2 other learners, however, problem behavior was low when the trainer provided attention but higher when the trainer made task demands, suggesting that the behaviors were related to task avoidance. Taylor et al. (1994) suggested that for some learners, certain types of social stimuli that are used during training, such as verbal and physical prompts and even praise, may actually elicit problem behaviors that are related to social avoidance. In such cases, a safety signal associated with termination of task demands would not be a very useful intervention procedure. Instead, the trainer might use fewer social stimuli initially and then gradually introduce these to assist the learner in tolerating social interaction over time.

Escape-motivated problem behavior may be related to variables such as task preference and difficulty, the amount and type of error correction used during training, the rate of instructional demands made during training, and even the duration of the training sessions. In addition to these variables, other more "remote" variables may influence problem behavior during training. It is important to consider these other types of variables, which can be viewed as motivational variables, also called establishing operations or setting events.

MOTIVATIONAL VARIABLES

There are three categories of motivational variables: biological, environmental, and social. Biological variables include the physical condition of the learner, such as illness or seizure activity, as well as effects of sleep deprivation, side effects of medication, altered mood states, hunger, or thirst. For example, a learner who is tired, ill, and hungry might be more irritable and, therefore, more likely to respond negatively to task demands by becoming upset and engaging in problem behavior. In some cases, biological variables may set the occasion for problem behavior. O'Reilly (1997), for example, showed that self-injury was related to ear infections in a young girl with developmental disability. In this case, self-injury occurred only when the child had otitis media. In other cases, a biological variable may exacerbate existing problem behavior. In another controlled case study, O'Reilly (1995) showed that the escape-motivated aggression of a 31-year-old man with developmental disability was more severe when the man had had a bad night's sleep.

Environmental variables may also directly evoke or indirectly exacerbate problem behaviors. Environmental variables may include the configuration of the training room, characteristics of the physical setting, noise levels, time of day, difficulty level of the task, and work or activity schedules. O'Reilly, Lacey, and Lancioni (2000) showed that increased background noise was associated with increased escape-maintained problem behavior in a 5-year-old girl with Williams syndrome. When the child wore earplugs to block the noise, her problem behavior decreased.

The third category of variables consists of a group of social conditions, such as the frequency and quality of social interactions and the presence or absence of specific individuals. For example, a learner might seek to escape from a task by engaging in problem behaviors when Bob is the trainer but not when Jody is running the training session. In such cases, the learner might simply prefer Jody and dislike Bob, but it might also be useful to observe the two trainers in action to see if there is an obvious reason for this difference. Perhaps, for example, Bob tends to reinforce escape behavior by terminating the task when problem behaviors occur, whereas Jody has extinguished such attempts. Alternatively, perhaps Bob may not provide enough reinforcement for task participation.

TREATMENT OF NEGATIVELY REINFORCED PROBLEM BEHAVIOR

Based on a consideration of biological, environmental, and social variables, three approaches to the treatment of escape-motivated problem behavior can be delineated. These approaches involve (a) alteration of the motivational variables, (b) use of antecedent control procedures, and (c) use of response-contingent and response-noncontingent procedures. These approaches are outlined in Table 5.1.

Alteration of Motivational Variables

Because an internal state or condition can influence problem behavior, it is considered an important type of motivational variable. Usually, a motivational variable interacts with environmental stimuli to increase the probability of problem behavior.

TABLE 5.1
Treatment of Negatively Reinforced Problem Behaviors

Alteration of Motivational Variables	Antecedent Control	Response Procedures
Neutralizing routines	Task fading	Differential reinforcement
Interspersed requests	Session fading	Training in functional ways of escape and requesting help
Physical exercise	Choice making	
Treatment of physical discomfort	Instructional procedures (errorless learning)	Guided compliance
		Noncontingent escape
Minimization of motivation variable's influence		Interruption prompting
		Noncontingent reinforcement
Positive context		
Environmental stimulation		

That is, problem behavior is more likely to occur in the presence of a specific discriminative stimulus (e.g., a task) when a certain state or condition also exists (e.g., illness, sleep deprivation, hunger). Therefore, one way to reduce the probability of problem behavior is to address the motivational variable (e.g., by treating the learner's illness or sleep problem).

In an attempt to alter motivational variables, Horner, Day, and Day (1997) inserted a neutralizing routine between the motivational variable and the discriminative stimulus for problem behavior. The procedure was used in the context of various instructional activities (e.g., writing, instruction following, sight-word reading). The authors collected data on motivational variables and discriminative stimuli that appeared to influence problem behavior. Examples of identified motivational variables included having to wait for a preferred activity and having less than 5 hours of sleep the previous night. Examples of discriminative stimuli included the trainer's making error corrections (e.g., saying, "That is wrong") and physically preventing the learner from reaching for a food item. An initial observation showed that problem behaviors were more likely to occur when both the motivational variable and the discriminative stimulus were present than when either one occurred alone. To reduce problem behaviors, the authors used a neutralizing routine prior to the instructional session. For example, one learner was given the opportunity to engage in a highly preferred activity prior to the instructional session. Engaging in the highly preferred activity was viewed by the authors as a way of neutralizing the aversiveness of the subsequent instructional session. Use of this neutralizing routine was effective in reducing the probability that problem behavior would occur during the subsequent instructional session.

If a learner's escape behaviors appear to be related to a nonpreferred task, then the trainer might reduce problem behavior by making the task less aversive. One way to do this is to insert a number of more preferred or easier routines into the task (Horner, Day, Sprague, O'Brien, & Heathfield, 1991). For example, after every instructional trial, the learner might be given an opportunity to request a preferred item. This procedure, known as interspersed requests, should make the task less aversive because the learner is given frequent opportunities to gain reinforcement for performing a simple request. The goal here is to make sure that the embedded activity is easy enough that the learner will respond quickly and correctly and hence gain reinforcement.

Another way to make a task less aversive is to intersperse some conversation not related to the task. Carr et al. (1976) attempted to reduce the aversive properties of instructional demands by having the trainers adopt a more cheerful and positive manner when interacting with the learners. For example, the trainer paused during training to tell a story in a cheerful manner. This procedure resulted in near-zero rates of problem behavior during training.

In some cases, as we have mentioned, problem behavior may be related to environmental variables. Duker and Rasing (1989) studied the relation between the physical complexity of the classroom and stereotypic behavior in 3 learners with autism. Stereotyped (or self-stimulatory) movements, which are common in children with autism and related developmental disabilities, include repetitive behaviors such as body rocking, head weaving, hand flapping, arm waving, and finger flicking. Stereotypy and time on task were assessed under conditions of high and low environmental stimulation—that is, in a normal classroom (high stimulation) and in a classroom from which many distracting materials were removed (low stimulation). As can be seen in Figure 5.2, a marked decrease in stereotypy and an increase in on-task behavior occurred during the treatment phases, when a low-stimulation classroom environment was created, as compared to the baseline phases, when the classroom was in its normal (high-stimulation) state. There was also an inverse relation between on-task behavior and stereotypy across all conditions.

So far, these types of relations between motivational variables and escape-motivated problem behavior suggest that trainers dealing with the analysis of problem behaviors should not ignore the potential influence of motivational variables. The influence of such variables, when they are shown to be relevant, might be minimized by altering or modifying the effects of the variable.

Antecedent Control

There is no clear distinction between manipulating a motivational variable and implementing an antecedent control procedure. These two types of procedures might best be viewed as two points along a continuum. Nevertheless, it may be worthy to discuss the more "nearby" antecedent events that control problem behavior during training separately from the more "distant" motivational variables.

Task or Demand Fading. One type of antecedent control procedure involves the gradual introduction, or fading in, of task demands. This procedure is indicated if problem behaviors are more likely when the task is difficult. In this situation, the trainer might begin with an easy task that does not evoke problem behavior. Over time (i.e., sessions), the trainer gradually introduces more difficult tasks while making sure that problem behaviors remain low. An important component

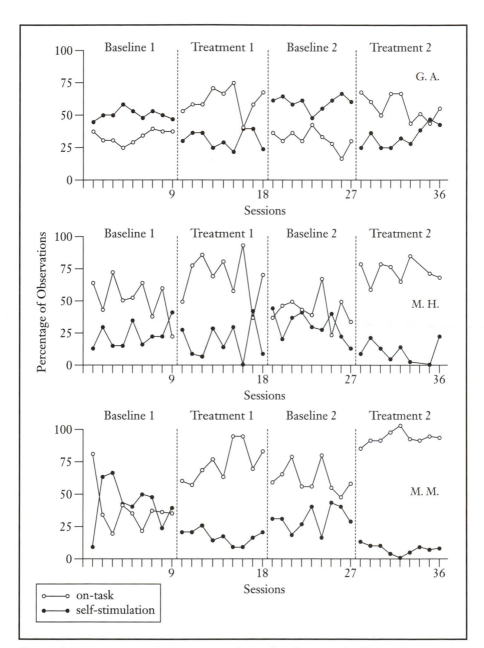

Figure 5.2. Percentage of observations of on-task behavior and self-stimulation.
Note. From "Effects of Redesigning the Physical Environment on Self-Stimulation and On-Task Behavior in Three Autistic-Type Developmentally Disabled Individuals," by P. Duker and E. Rasing, 1989, *Journal of Autism and Developmental Disorders, 19,* pp. 449–460. Copyright 1989 by Plenum Publishing. Reprinted with permission.

of this procedure is that the learner is taught the skills to cope with the increasingly more difficult tasks during one-to-one instruction.

A variation of this task-fading procedure is used when the learner's problem behaviors are related to the duration of the task demands. This technique is indicated, for example, when the learner works on a task for a few minutes, but then begins to demonstrate escape-motivated problem behavior. It is almost as if the learner is saying, "I have had enough of this." In this situation, the trainer begins by having only very short sessions. If the learner typically begins to engage in problem behavior after 5 minutes, then the initial sessions might be 3 minutes long. Over time, the length of the sessions is gradually increased so that the learner tolerates longer and longer training sessions. Smith et al. (1995), for example, found evidence suggesting that learners who showed an accelerating rate of problem behavior during a training session benefitted from brief, but more frequent, training sessions.

Pace, Iwata, Cowdery, Andree, and McIntyre (1993) described a task- or demand-fading procedure to decrease escape-motivated self-injury in 3 learners with developmental disabilities. In this case, the problem behaviors seemed to be related to the pace of instructional prompts during motor imitation, discrimination tasks, simple assembly, and sign language training. That is, high rates of self-injury were observed when the trainer presented instructional trials at the rate of once every 30 seconds, whereas no self-injury occurred when the rate of instructional trials was 0 per minute. Pace et al. (1993) gradually increased the rate of instructional prompts from 0 per minute to 2 per minute over a number of sessions. They also used an escape-extinction procedure—that is, instruction continued even if self-injury occurred. Self-injury decreased to near zero with each learner with the demand-fading procedure. In addition, each learner showed a marked increase in the rate of compliance to instructions. The results indicate that an antecedent control procedure involving task or demand fading may increase the effectiveness of other procedures, such as extinction, in the treatment of escape-motivated problem behavior during one-to-one training.

Choice Making. Another antecedent control procedure involves incorporating choice making into training sessions. We discussed the beneficial effects of choice making in Chapter 4. In this section, we consider the effects of providing choice-making opportunities on the rate of problem behaviors during training. Dyer, Dunlap, and Winterling (1990) assessed the effects of choice making on the aggressive and self-injurious behavior of 3 learners with developmental disabilities. The study was conducted in the context of instructional sessions to teach prevocational and preacademic skills. Observations of problem behaviors and task participation were conducted under two conditions. In the choice condition, the learner was provided with opportunities to choose from the available tasks. In the no-choice condition, the same tasks were provided but the trainer decided which task to use. The choice-making condition was associated with lower rates of problem behavior. Other studies have found that opportunities for choice making are associated with lower rates of problem behavior (see Sigafoos, 1998, for a review).

The opportunity to make choices and to indicate one's preferences could be viewed as a type of antecedent control procedure that may be effective in reducing problem behaviors. There could be at least two related reasons why this procedure might help to reduce problem behaviors during one-to-one training. First, choice making may function to decrease the aversive properties of a task or increase reinforcement because presumably the learner would choose the more preferred option. Second, choice making may eliminate the motivation for engaging in problem behavior to escape or avoid a task. That is, if the task is now associated with the opportunity to gain access to preferred options, then the learner may no longer be motivated to escape from this situation.

Sigafoos (1998) presented a model for the application of choice making as a type of antecedent control procedure. The model involves four steps, as shown in Figure 5.3. First, the trainer must identify how the learner will make a choice. Options include pointing, reaching for the object, using manual signs, or using some type of assistive communication device. If the learner does not have an appropriate way to make a choice,

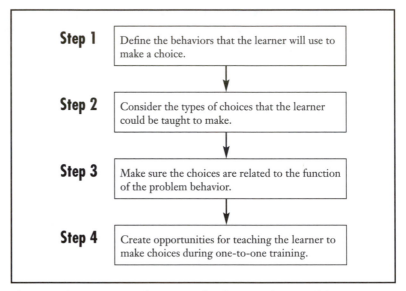

Figure 5.3. Steps in implementing the choice-making model.

then the procedures outlined in Chapters 1 and 2 are used to teach the choice-making response. This response should be easy and efficient for the learner to make. If the choice-making response is too difficult, then the learner is likely to continue to show problem behaviors to escape from or avoid the task.

Second, the trainer must identify occasions for choice making within the training session. These need to be related to the specific antecedents that set the occasion for problem behavior. If problem behaviors occur as soon as the task materials are presented, for example, then the trainer can give the learner a choice of materials at the beginning of the task, rather than merely presenting one set of materials. Alternatively, if the learner works at the task for a short time and then engages in problem behavior, it would make more sense to build in an opportunity to choose a break after a few minutes of work.

Third, the trainer must match choice-making opportunities to the function of the problem behavior. Learners may engage in problem behaviors to escape or avoid tasks, to gain attention, to access preferred objects, or for sensory stimulation. Choice-making opportunities that might help control object-motivated problem behavior include allowing the learner to choose among specific objects or activities, or letting the learner control the presentation and removal of these objects or activities. In contrast, the types of opportunities offered for escape-motivated problem behavior might include having the learner choose when and where to do the task, what materials to use, and how long to work at the task.

Fourth, the trainer needs to create explicit structured opportunities for choice making during instructional sessions. Learners with more severe disabilities may require concrete opportunities during which the trainer actually physically offers two or more items and allows the learner to point to the one he or she wants. Learners with good language comprehension skills, on the other hand, may respond to a verbally presented opportunity, such as "Do you want to take a break now or keep working?" Building choice opportunities into the learner's daily context is potentially useful as part of any instructional training session. Commonsense reasoning suggests that choice making is related to the quality of education and teaching (Lancioni, O'Reilly, & Emerson, 1996).

Errorless Learning. Errorless learning procedures may also be used to decrease problem behaviors that occur in response to difficult tasks or to error correction used during training. In a difficult task, the learner is likely to make more errors, which leads to more error correction and less frequent reinforcement. These conditions may set the occasion for problem behavior. With errorless learning procedures, the learner makes fewer errors, does not require as much error correction, and receives more frequent reinforcement. These procedures should lead to a reduction in problem behaviors.

In line with this logic, Weeks and Gaylord-Ross (1981) used an errorless learning procedure to teach a difficult visual discrimination. They first demonstrated that the difficult discrimination, which involved telling the difference between very similar geometric figures, was associated with high rates of errors and high rates of problem behaviors. They then reduced errors and, by consequence, problem behaviors by beginning with an easier discrimination and gradually making it more and more difficult, while making sure that at each step of the procedure the learners made no errors. Technically, their procedure involved stimulus shaping; that is, the incorrect stimulus card was gradually shaped to its final level in 10 steps, beginning with a blank card and progressing by adding more and more graphics to the card until it contained the complete geometric figure.

Response-Contingent and Response-Noncontingent Procedures

One of the problems with antecedent control procedures is that, theoretically, they would be expected to have little impact on the probability of occurrence of problem behavior once it has occurred. For example, if problem behavior occurs during training, and if it continues to enable the learner to escape from the task, then an antecedent control procedure by itself will not be sufficient to reduce problem behavior. For this reason, trainers will often need to combine antecedent control procedures with response-contingent or response-noncontingent procedures. A variety of these procedures can be used to reduce problem behaviors that occur during training.

The goal of response-contingent procedures is to modify the contingency between problem behavior and escape from the task. The idea is to make sure that problem behavior is no longer reinforced, that is, that it no longer enables the learner to escape from the task. One way to do this is to use an escape extinction procedure. Iwata, Pace, Kalsher, Cowdery, and Cataldo (1990) assessed the effects of escape extinction on the escape-motivated self-injurious behavior of 6 learners. An initial functional analysis revealed that the rate of self-injurious behavior was highest during the demand condition for each learner, indicating that these behaviors were related to task demands and probably maintained by the negative reinforcement of escape from those task demands. During one-to-one training, the trainer presented one instructional trial every 30 seconds. The tasks used during training included completing a jigsaw puzzle, pointing to pictures, and sorting objects. Correct responses were followed by praise, and errors were corrected using physical guidance. Treatment involving escape extinction was implemented by making sure that self-injury no longer enabled the learner to escape from the task. This procedure produced significant reductions in self-injury and increased participation in the task.

Another response-contingent procedure, called interruption prompting, has proven to be effective in the treatment of high-rate stereotypic behavior during task activities in the classroom (Duker & Schaapveld, 1996). Stereotyped behaviors may function as an escape response. With this procedure, the trainer briefly interrupted the learner's stereotypic behavior using physical restraint when it occurred and then prompted or redirected the learner to return to the task using a least-to-most prompting hierarchy. This procedure was associated with significant decreases in stereotypic behavior and increases in on-task behavior.

Extinction and guided compliance can be combined with functional communication training, in which the learner is taught to communicate as an alternative to problem behavior. For example, if the learner tries to escape from the task because it is too difficult, then he or she might be taught to request help with the task (Carr & Durand, 1985). In contrast, if the learner works on the task but then tries to escape using problem behavior, the learner might be taught to request a break from the task. In other words, the communicative behavior is made functionally equivalent to the problem behavior. Functional communication training involves teaching a learner to emit a communicative response (perhaps a manual sign, or pointing to a picture on a communication board) that belongs to the same response class as the problem behavior. Both the communicative behavior and the problem behavior are, therefore, likely to be controlled by the same discriminative stimulus or setting event.

In some cases functional communication training might not work, in that the problem behavior does not decrease even though the learner acquires the communicative alternative. One way to conceptualize this problem is that it reflects the operation of concurrent schedules of reinforcement. Functional communication training may be ineffective if the problem behavior requires less effort and produces more immediate reinforcement than the newly acquired communicative response. In such cases functional communication training may be combined with an extinction or aversive control procedure to effect a decrease in problem behavior. For example, Hagopian, Fisher, Sullivan, Acquisto, and LeBlanc (1998) taught 4 learners to use a communicative response to request a break from a task. However, problem behavior was reduced only when escape extinction or contingent manual restraint was added to the functional communication training procedure.

Reinforcement can also be delivered on a fixed-time schedule and irrespective of whether or not a problem behavior has occurred during or at the end of that interval. This is noncontingent reinforcement (NCR) because reinforcement is delivered irrespective of behavior. NCR is a relatively simple procedure because the trainer only has to remember to deliver reinforcement once every minute, or once every 5 minutes, or once every 10 minutes. For example, if the learner engages in escape-motivated tantrums during one-to-one training, the trainer may decide to deliver a break from the task initially every minute. This could be viewed as a type of noncontingent negative reinforcement, with the negative reinforcer being the break from the task. Over sessions, the amount of time between each noncontingent break can be gradually increased so that the learner works longer and longer before requiring a break. Moving from a break every minute to one only every 20 minutes, for example, might occur by increasing the interval by 1 minute after each session, provided that problem behavior remained low.

Vollmer, Marcus, and Ringdahl (1995) showed that this type of noncontingent escape from training was effective in reducing self-injury in 2 learners with profound disabilities. In these 2 individuals, the self-injury was first shown to be a form of escape behavior. Noncontingent escape seems to be a very useful procedure for reducing escape-motivated problem behaviors during one-to-one instruction. This procedure is perhaps most effective in situations where learners try to escape from the task because they want a break from task demands.

SUMMARY AND CONCLUSION

In this chapter, we have considered how to manage problem behaviors that occur during one-to-one training. Many such problem behaviors appear to be related to task demands and can be conceptualized as a form of escape or avoidance behavior. Learners might acquire and maintain escape behavior if the trainer typically has stopped the task when problem behavior occurred. There may be several reasons why the learner finds escape from the task reinforcing, including these possibilities: the task is too difficult, the task has gone on for too long, the learner does not like the task or the trainer, or some more preferred alternative has suddenly become available. Knowing which of these variables are relevant in any particular case can greatly assist trainers in designing effective treatment procedures.

Incorporating effective procedures to manage problem behaviors is often a necessary part of one-to-one training. Fortunately, a variety of effective treatment procedures have been developed to manage problem behaviors that occur during one-to-one training. These procedures include altering motivational variables, use of antecedent control procedures, and use of response-contingent and response-noncontingent procedures. Although other effective procedures are available, this chapter has attempted to outline a number of procedures and approaches that can be incorporated into one-to-one training. Careful selection and implementation of such procedures should enable trainers to effectively manage problem behaviors that occur during training.

Chapter 6

◆◆◆◆◆◆◆◆◆◆◆◆◆◆◆◆◆◆◆◆◆◆◆◆◆◆◆◆◆◆◆

Maintenance and Generalization

n addition to response acquisition, maintenance and generalization are two important outcomes of effective one-to-one training. Maintenance is the continued use of newly acquired responses after training is completed. Generalization is the use of responses acquired during one-to-one training in situations outside of the training environment, in other appropriate settings, with other people, and with other materials. Implementation of procedures to promote generalization and maintenance of training effects is therefore an important consideration when designing instructional programs for learners with developmental disabilities. The purpose of this chapter is to review procedures that can be used to promote maintenance and generalization of responses acquired during one-to-one training.

Implementing empirically validated procedures for promoting maintenance and generalization is important because it has been well documented that maintenance and generalization often do not occur in learners with developmental disabilities. Trainers hope that maintenance and generalization will occur, but these outcomes remain elusive in many instances, especially in training programs involving individuals with more severe disabilities (e.g., Duker & Jutten, 1997).

It is tempting for trainers to attribute the failure to maintain and generalize newly acquired responses to some deficit in the learner. It is often said that the learner has failed to maintain the response or that the learner has failed to generalize. However, sometimes the learner's so-called failure is due to the instructional procedures. Some training programs may be deficient in that they do not include procedures to promote maintenance and generalization. In fact, the conditions in effect during many training sessions may actually thwart maintenance and inhibit generalization. Many training programs include procedures that make generalization unlikely to occur because, during training, newly acquired responses are brought under the control of stimuli that do not occur outside of the training situation. In other cases, the natural environment has not been sufficiently prepared to ensure that newly acquired responses will enable the learner to gain reinforcement, so the responses are not maintained once training ends. In any event, because of the often noted lack of maintenance and generalization, trainers need to implement additional procedures during and after training to promote maintenance and generalization.

Several empirically validated procedures can be used to promote maintenance and generalization in learners with developmental disabilities. However, before considering some of these procedures in detail, we will explain the basic learning processes that underlie generalization and maintenance.

Let us first consider the issue of generalization. If training is conducted in a specific room with one set of instructional materials, then in addition to learning the response, the learner may also be learning to respond only in that setting and only when those materials are present. In a new setting with slightly different materials, it may appear as if the learner has forgotten what to do. Far from evidencing a memory problem, however, the learner may instead be showing that his or her responses have come under the control of the training situation and the stimuli associated with the training. Thus, the rather highly structured contexts in which many one-to-one training programs are conducted, while often necessary for response acquisition, may in fact work to undermine maintenance and generalization.

The noted lack of maintenance and generalization is not inevitable. It is not uncommon for a learner who has learned to request a drink in the presence of a blue cup, for example, to use this same requesting response in the presence of a red or a yellow cup, and to use the newly acquired requesting response in different settings and with different trainers. In such cases, one can say that the requesting response has generalized to novel stimuli. Of course, for this generalization to occur, one must assume that the learner is equally motivated to request a drink whether the cup is blue, red, or yellow. Some problems in generalization and maintenance may, therefore, reflect problems in motivation rather than a problem of stimulus control (Drasgow, Halle, & Sigafoos, 1999).

When stimulus control is narrow or limited to a few stimuli, generalization is unlikely to be as extensive as it would be if training involved a much wider range of stimuli, settings, and trainers. When stimulus control is broad in the sense of involving a greater variety of stimulus materials, settings, and trainers, then one might expect more generalization to occur. According to Skinner (1953), "generalization is not an activity of the organism: it is simply a term which describes the fact that the control acquired by a stimulus is shared by other stimuli with common properties" (p. 134).

When a response acquired in the presence of one stimulus later occurs in the presence of other, similar stimuli, this is called stimulus generalization. Generalization is also evident when one response is reinforced and an increase occurs in the rate of one or more other and functionally equivalent responses without these being taught or reinforced. This is called response generalization. For example, imagine that a learner has been taught to request a preferred toy by pointing to it when it is offered. After this, if the learner also starts to request toys by pointing to pictures of the object on a communication board, then this might indicate that response generalization has occurred. Sigafoos, Didden, and O'Reilly (2003) obtained some evidence suggesting response generalization in a 3-year-old boy, Curt, who was blind and developmentally disabled. He was taught to use a voice-output communication aid (VOCA) to request various preferred foods, drinks, and toys. After mastering the use of the device, Curt began to request these same items by speaking their names (e.g., "juice," "biscuit"), which suggests that response generalization had occurred. However, it is important to note that once Curt began to speak, his speech was reinforced, so the demonstration of response generalization is contaminated with the effects of reinforcement.

Maintenance refers to the continued use of a newly acquired response after the training program has ended. Maintenance can, therefore, be thought of as generalization over time. A trainer needs to consider how to promote three types of generalization: (a) stimulus generalization, in which the same response occurs across a variety of settings, people, and stimuli; (b) response generalization, in which other appropriate and functionally equivalent responses are strengthened as a result of teaching the targeted response; and (c) maintenance or generalization over time, which means that the response is maintained for a considerable period of time (e.g., 6, 12, 18 months) and, most important, that the response is maintained in the absence of continued training.

In addition to teaching the target response, trainers should also focus on how to promote these three types of generalization. For example, suppose that a trainer has been highly successful in teaching a young learner with severe autism to make requests for preferred objects. In fact, suppose the learner has acquired 10 different communicative gestures to request various preferred foods, drinks, and toys. Now suppose that all of the training has occurred in a classroom by one teacher who used a set of 10 training objects (e.g., a toy truck, a storybook, raisins, apple juice). At the end of the training program, the learner reliably produces 1 of the 10 gestures each time he is asked, "What do you want?" Although it is possible that this learner might also begin to produce these same gesture requests under different and yet equally appropriate stimulus conditions, such as when he is at home with his parents, there is no guarantee that this type of stimulus generalization will occur. If generalization fails to occur, the training program has been incomplete. The trainer needs to actively teach the learner to generalize his skills.

One-to-one training typically focuses on the acquisition of responses. During and after the acquisition phase, training can and should focus on promoting generalization and maintenance by incorporating certain procedures into the training program. Although other procedures have been developed, this chapter focuses on the four procedures described by Stokes and Osnes (1989) because these seem to be most compatible with the one-to-one instructional procedures described in this book. These strategies are (a) use of existing functional contingencies, (b) reduction of instructional control, (c) use of an intermittent schedule of reinforcement, and (d) use of common stimuli.

USE OF EXISTING FUNCTIONAL CONTINGENCIES

A *contingency* consists of three terms—an antecedent stimulus, response, and consequence—that are temporally related to each other, as shown in Figure 6.1. A *functional contingency* involves these same three terms, but it also implies that the antecedent stimulus is a discriminative stimulus for the response, and that the consequence is a reinforcer for the response. A functional contingency holds when the antecedent stimulus and

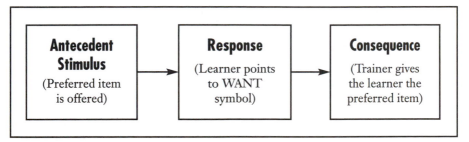

| Antecedent Stimulus (Preferred item is offered) | → | Response (Learner points to WANT symbol) | → | Consequence (Trainer gives the learner the preferred item) |

Figure 6.1. Example of a three-term contingency for teaching an initial requesting response.

consequence actually affect the rate, magnitude, or duration of the response.

From a generalization point of view, it is advantageous if the newly acquired response is actually part of a functional contingency that would be useful in various typical environments. For example, a learner might be taught to tap the table to request a drink during snack time in the classroom. This response is not very functional, however, because outside of the classroom no one would know that tapping the table means "I want a drink." A more functional response would have been to teach the child to operate a VOCA that produces a message such as "I want a drink of water, please." This response is more likely to form part of a functional contingency that will prove effective for the learner outside of the training environment. As a result, when the response occurs, other people will be more likely to reinforce it—by giving the child a drink of water—and hence the response is more likely to maintain and generalize because it has been reinforced in the natural environment. A standard guideline that pervades all aspects of training is to teach functional responses.

Horner (1971) investigated whether functional contingencies enhance generalization. He taught a 5-year-old boy with developmental and physical disabilities to use crutches as a way of increasing the child's independence in mobility. The child learned to use crutches in a training room. After learning this new skill, the boy was assessed in the use of his newly acquired mode of mobility in other settings where he had previously used only a wheelchair. Within 2 weeks after training, he was using the crutches in all of these settings. This generalization across settings was attributed to the fact that using crutches was a more functional mode of getting around. The use of crutches was reinforced by natural consequences, in that they enabled the child to get around his environment more efficiently.

Sometimes a newly acquired response does not generalize to the natural environment because it simply does not occur at a sufficiently high rate to make contact with the natural reinforcing consequences. For example, if a learner used a newly acquired response outside of training one time, but the staff did not notice, the response would not be reinforced. If the learner used the response more frequently or persisted with the response a few more times, the staff might notice and reinforce at least some instances of the response. Therefore, it may help to ensure that the response occurs frequently and persistently.

The tendency to repeat or persist with a response until reinforcement occurs is an important dimension of responding that can often be developed by simply overtraining the response. Unfortunately, most training programs end when the learner meets some minimal acquisition criteria (e.g., 80% correct over three consecutive sessions). After this, training moves on to a new response. As a result, the learner often has little opportunity to practice the response and build fluency. One way to promote greater fluency would be to continue training, perhaps by extending the acquisition criteria to 90% correct over at least 10 consecutive sessions. This procedure is known as overtraining. During overtraining, the trainer should occasionally not reinforce the response until the learner repeats the response. This procedure of intermittent reinforcement should also make the behavior more resistant to extinction and, therefore, more likely to be maintained after training.

In addition to using overtraining and intermittent reinforcement, the trainer should increase contact with the natural functional contingencies by using a procedure that involves "actively recruiting natural consequences" (Stokes & Osnes, 1989). Mank and Horner (1987) used this procedure with 6 learners with developmental disabilities who were taught to self-monitor their work performance and productivity. They were also taught to compare their performance with a criterion and then to solicit feedback about their performance from their supervisors. Thus, the procedure involved teaching the learners to recruit an audience for their responses so that the audience would then deliver reinforcing consequences.

REDUCTION OF INSTRUCTIONAL CONTROL

Another procedure for promoting generalization is to reduce the amount of control over the stimuli that are used during training. This approach is based on the assumption that the use of a precise training procedure, which specifies what the trainer should do and say, the stimuli that should be used, and the configuration of the training arrangement, may reduce generalization by bringing the response under overly precise stimulus control. For example, if training always occurs in only one setting, perhaps a training room with a single table and chairs, then it is perhaps less likely that the responses acquired in this room would occur in other settings. In contrast, if training occurs at home, in the classroom, and in the community, then there is perhaps a greater chance of establishing generalization across settings. This is because training has occurred in multiple settings, which vary in terms of the stimuli that are present during training. Conducting training in multiple settings is just one way to reduce instructional control and broaden stimulus control.

Stokes and Osnes (1989) described two strategies that a trainer might use to reduce instructional control so as to promote generalization. These two techniques are to (a) use sufficient stimulus and response exemplars and (b) train loosely.

Use of Sufficient Exemplars

Stimulus Exemplars. A stimulus exemplar is simply some discrete aspect of the training protocol. It could be the room, the materials presented, or the person who does the training. The idea is to use a variety of exemplars, such as a variety of rooms, a variety of materials, and more than one trainer. In addition, the variety of stimuli should reflect the range of variation that is actually found across environments (Horner & Albin, 1988).

If multiple stimulus exemplars are involved in the training, better generalization is to be expected than if only one stimulus exemplar is employed. For example, Haring (1985) taught children with disabilities to play with various toys. Training focused on the use of toy-specific play behaviors, such as holding and moving an airplane through the air. As part of the training, the children were exposed to a variety of toys (i.e., multiple stimulus exemplars). After training, the children's newly acquired play skills generalized to a number of other toys that were not part of the training. Generalization of play skills to novel untrained toys was attributed to the use of multiple stimulus exemplars during training.

It is difficult to know in advance how many exemplars will be sufficient for generalization to occur. Stokes, Baer, and Jackson (1974), for example, found that if only one trainer taught a greeting response to learners with developmental disabilities, generalization to other adults did not occur. However, if two trainers taught the response, then it generalized to direct-care staff members who had not participated in the training. Garcia (1974) also found that using two trainers was sufficient to ensure generalization to other staff. This study systematically replicates the results of Stokes et al. (1974) in that it targeted conversational speech in 2 children with developmental disability.

Response Exemplars. In explaining response generalization, it is important to emphasize the notion of response class. A response class refers to a set of topographically distinct responses that nonetheless are functionally equivalent. For example, saying "Drink" is different from making the manual sign for "drink," yet the two responses may both function as a request for a drink. Therefore, both response forms would properly be classified as members of the same response class. A response class consists of all the responses that produce or are maintained by the same consequences. A procedure, such as reinforcement, that is applied to one member of the response class may affect other members of the response class.

The study by Baer, Peterson, and Sherman (1967) may help to clarify the concept of response class. Baer et al. initially taught learners with developmental disabilities to imitate various motor acts. They found that as long as the students were reinforced following some imitative responses, the students acquired other imitative responses despite no reinforcement. These findings suggest not that the students had acquired merely a few motor responses, but rather that they had acquired motor imitation itself as a class of responses.

Unexpected results can be found in the area of generalization. For example, Carr and Kologinsky (1983) taught children with autism to request preferred objects using manual signs, but they found that as these signs were acquired, the learners' stereotyped movements decreased. The collateral decrease in one behavior as a function of increasing another behavior suggests that the two behaviors belonged to the same response class.

Loose Training

A variation of the use of sufficient exemplars is known as loose training. Loose training is based on the idea that generalization will be more likely to occur to novel stimuli if training involves a broad range of stimuli and if trainers are not too precise in how they present materials and deliver prompts. Campbell and Stremel-Campbell (1982) used this procedure in teaching 2 learners with developmental delays to increase their use of certain syntactic structures, such as the appropriate use of "is" and "are" in response to a trainer's questions. The training conditions allowed the learner to initiate a verbal response in the presence of a wide array of natural stimuli or to respond to the trainer's prompts, questions, or statements as an attempt to broaden the stimulus control of these responses. Any correct response that occurred under these various conditions was reinforced using social consequences and tokens. Generalization was assessed in a free-play setting, in which the children were encouraged to engage in activities of their choice and to engage in conversations with peers and teachers in the classroom. The results showed that there was generalization of the newly acquired verbal responses. This generalization was attributed to the fact that during training, the children learned to respond with the correct verbal responses to a variety of cues, including a variety of verbal prompts by the trainer, such as "What do you want?" "What's next?" and "Is there anything you want?"

USE OF INTERMITTENT REINFORCEMENT

Another procedure that might be used to promote maintenance and generalization is to make consequences less distinguishable for the learner. Intermittent schedules of reinforcement, especially variable ratio and variable interval schedules, have been shown to increase resistance to extinction. We mentioned intermittent reinforcement previously when considering the issue of overtraining. In the current context, it is important to explore the issue in more detail. Resistance to extinction refers, in part, to how long a learner will continue to respond in the absence of reinforcement. Generally, the more resistant a response is to extinction, the more likely it is that that response will be maintained. During one-to-one training, each and every correct response may be reinforced. Outside of the training situation, however, an appropriate or correct response may not always be reinforced. Indeed, responses that received consistent reinforcement during training may obtain only occasional reinforcement outside of the training environment. In other words, the schedule of reinforcement is mainly continuous during training, but the schedule is typically more intermittent outside of the training environment. If every response is reinforced, a continuous reinforcement schedule is in effect. On the other hand, if not every response is reinforced, but on average only every 4th, 10th, or 20th response is reinforced, some type of intermittent schedule, in this case a variable ratio schedule, is in effect. Therefore, if the schedule of reinforcement during training is made more intermittent, it is more likely to match the prevailing contingencies in natural settings, and hence the response is more likely to be maintained in those settings.

Koegel and Rincover (1977) studied the manipulation of the schedule of reinforcement for promoting maintenance. They taught learners with autism to imitate various responses and complete various instructional tasks in a training setting. They then assessed stimulus generalization and maintenance in other settings. They found that although the responses initially generalized to other settings, they were not maintained. When they then shifted to the use of intermittent reinforcement—that is, gradually thinning the schedule of reinforcement from continuous to providing reinforcement for only every sixth response on average (i.e., variable ratio 6)—they obtained maintenance.

In another study of the use of intermittent reinforcement to promote maintenance, Kazdin and Polster (1973) reinforced the social interactions of 2 learners with developmental disabilities during break periods in a sheltered workshop. They compared the effects of two reinforcement schedules on response maintenance under conditions of extinction. The basic finding was that social interactions were better maintained when reinforced on a more intermittent, rather than a continuous, schedule of reinforcement.

Use of intermittent reinforcement schedules can pose a timing problem during the initial stages of training. Because response acquisition often requires continuous reinforcement to strengthen the response during the early stages of training, the trainer needs to consider when and how to shift to a more intermittent schedule of reinforcement. Unfortunately, there are no clear guidelines for this. Generally, the idea is for the learner's response level to reach the initial acquisition criteria using continuous reinforcement, and then for the trainer to shift gradually to a more intermittent schedule of reinforcement during the overtraining phase of instruction. However, even if the learner has reached initial acquisition criteria (e.g., 80% correct over three consecutive sessions), trainers often continue to use a continuous schedule of reinforcement. Sustaining this reinforcement level may cause a problem, however, because outside of the training situation, continuous reinforcement is not typical. The resulting contrast between the schedules of reinforcement operating in the training sessions and those operating at other times may be one reason for the failure of many newly acquired responses to maintain and generalize after training has ended. Trainers, therefore, should aim to introduce a schedule of reinforcement that matches the one that is found in the natural environment as part of the training program.

USE OF COMMON STIMULI

A common stimulus is one that is common to more than one setting. For instance, the stimulus might be found in both the training environment and the natural environment. A learner who is taught to respond in the presence of this stimulus during training may be more likely to respond in other nontraining situations where this same stimulus is present. At a practical level, the common stimulus might be something that can be carried by the learner to a variety of natural settings so that it is always present. For example, the learner might carry from place to place the set of graphic symbols related to performing a task. The pictures, line drawings, or symbols carried by the learner might function as common stimuli, thereby facilitating generalization and maintenance.

Pictorial instructional cues are a practical example of common stimuli. These cues, often presented on cards, are used to establish and maintain independent task performance across various settings, predominantly with learners with mild developmental disabilities (for a comprehensive review, see Lancioni & O'Reilly, 2001).

Charlop, Schreibman, and Thibodeau (1985) investigated the programming of common stimuli in a study on teaching learners with autism to name objects. The training stimuli were food and drinks, which were also the reinforcers for correct responding. When these same (i.e., common) stimuli were presented in other nontraining settings, the researchers found that the learners had generalized the newly acquired object labels to these other settings.

Possibly any stimulus, even verbal instructions given by teachers and direct-care staff, might come to function as common stimuli. Duker and Morsink (1984) assessed the generalization of communicative gestures from a training room to classroom and residential settings for learners with developmental disabilities. The common stimuli that were first used in the training room and then presented in the classroom and residence consisted of a set of verbal instructions given by teachers and direct-care staff. The use of these common verbal stimuli across settings resulted in generalization from the training setting to the classroom and residential settings. Others have attempted to make the training setting gradually resemble the generalization setting (i.e., the classroom) as a way of introducing common stimuli. Koegel and Rincover (1974), for example, did this by decreasing the 1:1 teacher-to-student ratio in the training setting to the more typical 1:8 ratio found in the learners' classrooms.

The weakness the concept of common stimuli is that its definition is based on a post hoc analysis of the learner's performance. That is, if generalization occurs, then the stimulus is defined as common, whereas if generalization does not occur, then the intended stimulus did not in fact operate as a common stimulus for generalization.

SUMMARY AND CONCLUSION

Three major expected outcomes from the type of one-to-one training outlined in this book are (a) response acquisition, (b) maintenance, and (c) generalization. Most training programs for learners with developmental disabilities end once the learner has acquired the response. Trainers often simply hope that the responses they have taught will be maintained by the learner and will generalize to other settings, materials, and people. Unfortunately, generalization and maintenance do not always spontaneously occur. Therefore, instead of hoping for maintenance and generalization, trainers should include additional instructional procedures to promote maintenance and generalization. Although a variety of such procedures exist, the basic principles are found in the four strategies outlined in this chapter (i.e., use of existing functional contingencies, reduction of instructional control, use of intermittent reinforcement, and use of common stimuli). Understanding the basic principles involved in the use of these procedures will enable trainers to be more successful at ensuring that the responses they have taught will continue to be useful to the learners once acquisition has occurred. Training is not complete until the responses that have been taught are maintained and generalized.

Glossary

antecedent stimulus. A stimulus that precedes a response.

backward chaining. An instructional procedure in which the last response of the behavior chain is trained first, and in which responses of the chain are added successively in the reverse sequence until the first response is trained.

behavior chain. A sequence of related responses—each of which provides the discriminative stimulus for the next response—that are successively reinforced.

concurrent schedules of reinforcement. A situation in which two or more reinforcement schedules operate simultaneously, each for a different response.

consequent stimulus. A stimulus that follows or is presented contingent on a response.

continuous schedule of reinforcement. A schedule of reinforcement in which each instance of a correct response is reinforced.

differential reinforcement. A procedure in which a specific response to one stimulus is reinforced, while the same response to another stimulus is not reinforced.

discrete trial training. Presentation of opportunities for a learner's response across a number of trials that are initiated by the trainer during a session.

discriminative stimulus. A stimulus that evokes a response and that has been associated with reinforcement of that response.

error correction. An instructional procedure in which an error is corrected or a forthcoming error is interrupted.

errorless learning. Use of instructional procedures that aim at ensuring the occurrence of only correct or few incorrect responses by the systematic fading of stimulus and response prompts.

establishing operation. An event or condition that temporarily alters a reinforcer's effectiveness and that increases the probability of occurrence of a response that is maintained by that reinforcer (also often called *setting event*).

extinction. A decrease in the probability of occurrence of a response by withholding the reinforcer of that response contingent upon its occurrence.

fading. The gradual reduction of prompts until the discriminative stimulus evokes the target response independently.

flowchart. A graphic display of the steps of an instructional procedure.

forward chaining. An instructional procedure in which the first response of the behavior chain is trained first, and responses are added successively in the sequence of the behavior chain until its last response is trained.

functional analysis. A set of procedures that test the (hypothesized) relation between the target response and its discriminative stimuli and maintaining consequences.

functional skill. A skill that is frequently used during a learner's daily routine and that would be expected to occur in the learner's natural setting(s).

graduated guidance. The fading of a trainer's physical prompts, during a trial or across a number of trials, by providing only as much physical assistance as is necessary for a learner to execute the response.

imitation. A type of observational learning that involves imitating a response that is observed in another person.

incidental teaching. Opportunities that are initiated by a learner's response in natural settings.

intermittent schedule of reinforcement. A schedule of reinforcement in which not every response is reinforced (included are time and ratio schedules).

interrupted behavior chain. Interruption of a learner's behavior chain to provide an opportunity for teaching communicative responses (i.e., requesting) to the learner.

interruption prompting. A (physical) prompt that interrupts an off-task response and redirects the learner to an on-task response.

learning. A relatively permanent change in a learner's behavioral repertoire as a result of repeated associations between target responses and their discriminative stimuli and reinforcers.

least-to-most prompting. An instructional procedure in which prompting proceeds from prompts providing less assistance to prompts providing more assistance (also called *procedure of increasing assistance*).

maintenance. The continued use of a newly learned response after the training program has ended.

mand. A verbal operant that is under control of primary or conditioned establishing operations in which the form of the response produces some characteristic type of consequence (e.g., requesting or rejecting).

most-to-least prompting. An instructional procedure in which prompting proceeds from prompts providing more assistance to prompts providing less assistance (also called *procedure of decreasing assistance*).

negative reinforcement. An increase in the probability of the future occurrence of a response by removing, avoiding, or postponing a stimulus contingent on that response.

operant conditioning. A type of learning in which the probability of the future occurrence of a response is increased or decreased as a result of its consequent stimuli.

overtraining. A continuation of the training of a response, even if the initial acquisition criterion has been met.

positive reinforcement. An increase in the probability of the future occurrence of a response by adding a stimulus contingent on that response.

preference assessment. A procedure in which a learner's relative preference for a stimulus is assessed compared to others in a pool of stimuli.

primary reinforcer. A consequent stimulus that strengthens a response with little or no prior learning (e.g., food).

prompt. An added stimulus that increases the probability that the target response will occur (included are stimulus and response prompts).

reinforcer. A consequent stimulus that increases or maintains the probability of the future occurrence of a response.

reinforcer assessment. Assessment of the reinforcing properties of a stimulus that was chosen as being preferred during preference assessment.

respondent conditioning. A type of learning in which a conditioned stimulus elicits a response by being paired repeatedly with an unconditioned stimulus that already elicits that response (also called *classical* or *Pavlovian conditioning*).

response class. A group of different responses that are maintained by the same reinforcer.

response delay. Prevention of a learner's response to a discriminative stimulus for a specific time interval.

response generalization. An unprogrammed change in other responses of the learner due to modification of a target response.

response latency. The time period between the presentation of a stimulus and a learner's response.

response restriction. An increase in the probability of occurrence of a response due to physically restricting other responses.

schedule of reinforcement. A rule that specifies how often and under what conditions a particular response will be reinforced (included are fixed and variable schedules of reinforcement).

session. A daily or weekly time period in which instructional procedures are individually implemented across trials.

shadowing. The physical monitoring by the trainer of a learner's response during its execution.

shaping. The differential reinforcement of successive approximations of a target response and extinction of preceding approximations.

stimulus control. The degree to which a discriminative stimulus sets the occasion for a target response.

stimulus generalization. The degree to which a specific response occurs in the presence of stimuli that are similar but not identical to the discriminative stimulus for that response.

stimulus overselectivity. The tendency to respond to only one stimulus if this stimulus is presented in a compound stimulus.

tact. A verbal operant that is controlled by a prior nonverbal stimulus that produces some type of generalized reinforcement (e.g., labeling, naming, describing).

task analysis. The process in which a task is broken down into smaller steps.

time delay. An increase in the time interval between a discriminative stimulus and a prompt until the learner's response occurs without prompting (includes constant and progressive time delay). (Also called *delayed cueing* and *delayed prompting*.)

total task training. An instructional procedure in which every response in a task is trained during successive trials.

trial. A discrete learning opportunity that involves a trainer-delivered opportunity, a learner response, and delivery of consequences for the learner's response.

References

◆◆◆◆◆◆◆◆◆◆◆◆◆◆◆◆◆◆◆◆◆◆◆◆◆◆◆◆

Ault, M. J., Gast, D. L., & Wolery, M. (1988). Comparison of progressive and constant time-delay procedures in teaching community-sign word reading. *American Journal on Mental Retardation, 93*, 44–56.

Azrin, N. H., & Armstrong, P. M. (1973). The "mini-meal"—A method for teaching eating skills to the profoundly retarded. *Mental Retardation, 11*, 9–11.

Azrin, N. H., Schaeffer, R. M., & Wesolowski, M. D. (1976). A rapid method of teaching profoundly retarded persons to dress by a reinforcement–guidance method. *Mental Retardation, 14*, 29–33.

Baer, D. M., Peterson, R. F., & Sherman, J. A. (1967). The development of imitation by reinforcing behavioral similarity to a model. *Journal of the Experimental Analysis of Behavior, 10*, 405–416.

Billingsley, F. F., & Romer, L. T. (1983). Response prompting and the transfer of stimulus control: Methods, research, and a conceptual framework. *The Journal of the Association for the Severely Handicapped, 8*, 3–12.

Bowman, L. G., Piazza, C. C., Fisher, W. W., Hagopian, L. P., & Kogan, J. S. (1997). Assessment of preference for varied versus constant reinforcers. *Journal of Applied Behavior Analysis, 30*, 451–458.

Braam, S. J., & Poling, A. (1983). Development of intraverbal behavior in mentally retarded individuals through transfer of stimulus control procedures: Classification of verbal responses. *Applied Research in Mental Retardation, 4*, 279–302.

Brady, N. C., & Halle, J. W. (2002). Breakdowns and repairs in conversations between beginning AAC users and their partners. In J. Reichle, D. R. Beukelman, & J. C. Light (Eds.), *Exemplary practices for beginning communicators: Implications for AAC* (pp. 323–351). Baltimore: Brookes.

Bucher, B. (1983). Effects of sign-language training on untrained sign use for single and multiple signing. *Analysis and Intervention in Developmental Disabilities, 3*, 261–277.

Campbell, C. R., & Stremel-Campbell, K. (1982). Programming "loose training" as a strategy to facilitate language generalization. *Journal of Applied Behavior Analysis, 15*, 292–301.

Carr, E. G., & Durand, V. M. (1985). Reducing behavior problems through functional communication training. *Journal of Applied Behavior Analysis, 18*, 111–126.

Carr, E. G., & Kologinsky, E. (1983). Acquisition of sign language by autistic children: II. Spontaneity and generalization effects. *Journal of Applied Behavior Analysis, 16*, 297–314.

Carr, E. G., & Newsom, C. D. (1985). Demand-related tantrums: Conceptualization and treatment. *Behavior Modification, 9*, 403–426.

Carr, E. G., Newsom, C. D., & Binkoff, J. A. (1976). Stimulus control of self-destructive behavior in a psychotic child. *Journal of Abnormal Child Psychology, 4*, 139–153.

Carr, E. G., Newsom, C. D., & Binkoff, J. A. (1980). Escape as a factor in the aggressive behavior of two retarded children. *Journal of Applied Behavior Analysis, 13*, 101–117.

Carr, E. G., Taylor, J. C., & Robinson, S. (1991). The effects of severe behavior problems in children on the teaching behaviors of adults. *Journal of Applied Behavior Analysis, 24*, 523–535.

Charlop, M. H., Schreibman, L., & Thibodeau, M. G. (1985). Increasing spontaneous verbal responding in autistic children using a time delay procedure. *Journal of Applied Behavior Analysis, 18*, 155–166.

Cronin, K. A., & Cuvo, A. J. (1979). Teaching mending skills to mentally retarded adolescents. *Journal of Applied Behavior Analysis, 12*, 401–406.

Csapo, M. (1981). Comparison of two prompting procedures to increase response fluency among handicapped learners. *The Journal of the Association for the Severely Handicapped, 6*, 39–45.

Cummins, R. A. (1991). The Comprehensive Quality of Life Scale–Intellectual Disability: An instrument under development. *Australia and New Zealand Journal of Developmental Disabilities, 17*, 259–264.

DeLeon, I., & Iwata, B. A. (1996). Evaluation of a multiple-stimulus presentation format for assessing reinforcer preferences. *Journal of Applied Behavior Analysis, 29*, 519–533.

Derby, K. M., Wacker, D. P., Sasso, G., Steege, M., Northup, J., Cigrand, K., & Asmus, J. (1992). Brief functional assessment techniques to evaluate aberrant behavior in an outpatient setting: A summary of 79 cases. *Journal of Applied Behavior Analysis, 25*, 713–721.

Didden, R., & de Moor, J. (2004). Preference assessment in toddlers with mild developmental and physical disabilities: A comparative study. *Journal of Developmental and Physical Disabilities, 16*, 107–116.

Didden, R., de Moor, J. M., & Bruyns, W. (1997). Effectiveness of DRO tokens in decreasing disruptive behaviors in the classroom with five multiply handicapped children. *Behavioral Interventions, 12*, 65–75.

Didden, R., Prinsen, H., & Sigafoos, J. (2000). The blocking effect of pictorial prompts on sight word reading. *Journal of Applied Behavior Analysis, 33*, 317–320.

Diorio, M. S., & Konarski, E. A. (1984). Evaluation of a method for teaching dressing skills to profoundly retarded persons. *American Journal of Mental Deficiency, 89*, 307–309.

Drasgow, E., Halle, J. W., Ostrosky, M. M., & Harbers, H. M. (1996). Using behavioral indication and functional communication training to establish an initial sign repertoire with a young child with severe disabilities. *Topics in Early Childhood Special Education, 16,* 500–521.

Drasgow, E., Halle, J., & Sigafoos, J. (1999). Teaching communication to learners with severe disabilities: Motivation, response competition, and generalization. *Australasian Journal of Special Education, 23,* 47–63.

Duker, P. (1981). Prevention of incorrect responding for establishing instruction following behaviors. *Journal of Mental Deficiency Research, 25,* 25–32.

Duker, P. (1988). *Teaching the developmentally handicapped communicative gesturing: A how-to-do book.* Berwyn, PA: Swets North American.

Duker, P., Averink, M., & Melein, L. (2001). Response restriction as a method to establish diurnal bladder control. *American Journal of Mental Retardation, 106,* 209–215.

Duker, P., Dortmans, E., & Lodder, E. (1993). Establishing the manding function of communicative gestures with individuals with severe/profound mental retardation. *Research in Developmental Disabilities, 14,* 39–49.

Duker, P., & Jutten, W. (1997). Establishing gestural yes–no responding with individuals with profound mental retardation. *Education and Training in Mental Retardation and Developmental Disabilities, 32,* 59–67.

Duker, P., Kraaykamp, M., & Visser, E. (1994). A stimulus control procedure to increase requesting with individuals who are severely/profoundly intellectually disabled. *Journal of Intellectual Disability Research, 38,* 177–186.

Duker, P., & Michielsen, H. (1983). Cross-setting generalization of manual signs to verbal instructions with severely retarded children. *Applied Research in Mental Retardation, 4,* 29–40.

Duker, P., & Morsink, H. (1984). Acquisition and cross-setting generalization of manual signs with severely retarded individuals. *Journal of Applied Behavior Analysis, 17,* 93–103.

Duker, P., & Rasing, E. (1989). Effects of redesigning the physical environment on self-stimulation and on-task behavior in three autistic-type developmentally disabled individuals. *Journal of Autism and Developmental Disorders, 19,* 449–460.

Duker, P., & Schaapveld, M. (1996). Increasing on-task behaviour through interruption-prompting. *Journal of Intellectual Disability Research, 40,* 291–297.

Duker, P., van Deursen, W., de Wit, M., & Palmen, A. (1997). Establishing a receptive repertoire of communicative gestures with individuals who are profoundly mentally retarded. *Education and Training in Mental Retardation and Developmental Disabilities, 32,* 357–361.

Duker, P., van Doeselaar, C., & Verstraten, A. (1993). The effect of response delay on correct responding to instructions during communicative gesture training. *Education and Training in Mental Retardation, 28*, 327–332.

Duker, P., & van Lent, C. (1991). Inducing variability in communicative gestures used by severely retarded individuals. *Journal of Applied Behavior Analysis, 24*, 379–386.

Dunlap, G., DePerczel, M., Clark, S., Wilson, D., Wright, S., White, R., & Gomez, A. (1994). Choice making to promote adaptive behavior for students with emotional and behavioral challenges. *Journal of Applied Behavior Analysis, 27*, 505–518.

Durand, V. M., & Carr, E. G. (1987). Social influences on "self-stimulatory" behavior: Analysis and treatment implications. *Journal of Applied Behavior Analysis, 20*, 119–132.

Dyer, K., Christian, W. P., & Luce, S. C. (1982). The role of response delay in improving the discrimination performance of autistic children. *Journal of Applied Behavior Analysis, 15*, 231–240.

Dyer, K., Dunlap, G., & Winterling, V. (1990). Effects of choice-making on the serious problem behaviors of students with severe handicaps. *Journal of Applied Behavior Analysis, 23*, 515–524.

Egel, A. L. (1981). Reinforcer variation: Implications for motivating developmentally disabled children. *Journal of Applied Behavior Analysis, 14*, 345–350.

Fisher, W. W., Piazza, C. C., Bowman, L. G., & Amari, A. (1996). Integrating caregiver report with a systematic choice assessment to enhance reinforcer identification. *American Journal on Mental Retardation, 101*, 15–25.

Fisher, W. W., Piazza, C. C., Bowman, L. G., Hagopian, L. P., Owens, J. C., & Slevin, I. (1992). A comparison of two approaches for identifying reinforcers for persons with severe and profound disabilities. *Journal of Applied Behavior Analysis, 25*, 491–498.

Foxx, R. M., McMorrow, M. J., Faw, G. D., Kyle, M. S., & Bittle, R. G. (1987). Cues–pause–point language training: Structuring trainer statements to students with correct answers to questions. *Behavioral Residential Treatment, 2*, 103–115.

Garcia, E. (1974). The training and generalization of a conversational speech form in nonverbal retardates. *Journal of Applied Behavior Analysis, 7*, 137–149.

Gast, D. L., Ault, M. J., Wolery, M., Doyle, P. M., & Belanger, S. (1988). Comparison of constant time delay and system of least prompts in teaching sight word reading to students with moderate mental retardation. *Education and Treatment in Mental Retardation, 23*, 117–128.

Gaylord-Ross, R. J., Weeks, M., & Lipner, C. (1980). An analysis of antecedent, response, and consequent events in the treatment of self-injurious behavior. *Education and Training of the Mentally Retarded, 5*, 35–42.

Giangreco, M. F. (1983). Teaching basic photography skills to a severely handicapped young adult using simulated materials. *Journal of the Association for the Severely Handicapped, 8,* 43–49.

Gold, M. W. (1972). Stimulus factors in skill training of the retarded on a complex assembly task: Acquisition, transfer, and retention. *American Journal of Mental Deficiency, 76,* 517–526.

Green, C. W., Reid, D. H., Canipe, V. S., & Gardner, S. M. (1991). A comprehensive evaluation of reinforcer identification processes for persons with profound multiple handicaps. *Journal of Applied Behavior Analysis, 24,* 537–552.

Green, C. W., Reid, D. H., White, L. K., Halford, R. C., Brittain, D. P., & Gardner, S. M. (1988). Identifying reinforcers for persons with profound handicaps: Staff opinion versus systematic assessment of preferences. *Journal of Applied Behavior Analysis, 21,* 31–43.

Haavik, S., & Altman, K. (1977). Establishing walking by severely retarded children. *Perceptual and Motor Skills, 44,* 1107–1114.

Hagopian, L. P., Fisher, W. W., Sullivan, M. T., Acquisto, J., & LeBlanc, L. A. (1998). Effectiveness of functional communication training with and without extinction and punishment: A summary of 21 inpatient cases. *Journal of Applied Behavior Analysis, 31,* 211–235.

Halle, J. W. (1987). Teaching language in the natural environment: An analysis of spontaneity. *Journal of the Association for Persons with Severe Handicaps, 12,* 28–37.

Halle, J. W., Marshall, A. M., & Spradlin, J. E. (1979). Time delay: A technique to increase language use and facilitate generalization in retarded children. *Journal of Applied Behavior Analysis, 12,* 431–439.

Haring, T. G. (1985). Teaching between-class generalization of toy play behavior to handicapped children. *Journal of Applied Behavior Analysis, 19,* 127–139.

Hoogeveen, F., Smeets, P. M., & Lancioni, G. E. (1989). Teaching moderately mentally retarded children basic reading skills. *Research in Developmental Disabilities, 10,* 1–18.

Hoogeveen, F., Smeets, P. M., & van der Houven, J. E. (1987). Establishing letter–sound correspondences in children classified as trainable mentally retarded. *Education and Training in Mental Retardation, 22,* 77–84.

Horner, R. D., & Keilitz, I. (1975). Training mentally retarded adolescents to brush their teeth. *Journal of Applied Behavior Analysis, 8,* 301–309.

Horner, R. H. (1971). Establishing use of crutches by a mentally retarded spina bifida child. *Journal of Applied Behavior Analysis, 4,* 183–189.

Horner, R. H., & Albin, R. W. (1988). Research on general-case procedures for learners with severe disabilities. *Education and Treatment of Children, 11,* 375–388.

Horner, R. H., Day, M. H., & Day, J. R. (1997). Using neutralizing routines to reduce problem behaviors. *Journal of Applied Behavior Analysis, 30,* 601–614.

Horner, R. H., Day, M. H., Sprague, J. R., O'Brien, M., & Heathfield, L. T. (1991). Interspersed requests: A nonaversive procedure for decreasing aggression and self-injury during instruction. *Journal of Applied Behavior Analysis, 24,* 265–278.

Houlihan, D., Jones, R., & Sloane, H. (1992). The simultaneous presentation procedure: Use in selecting reinforcers for behavioral intervention. *Education and Treatment of Children, 15,* 244–254.

Ivancic, M. C., & Bailey, J. S. (1996). Current limits to reinforcer identification for some people with profound multiple disabilities. *Research in Developmental Disabilities, 17,* 77–92.

Iwata, B. A., Pace, G. M., Dorsey, M., Zarcone, J., Vollmer, T., Smith, R., Rodgers, T., Lerman, D. C., Shore, B., Mazaleski, J., Goh, H., Cowdery, G. E., Kalsher, M. J., McCosh, K., & Willis, K. (1994). The functions of self-injurious behavior: An experimental–epidemiological analysis. *Journal of Applied Behavior Analysis, 27,* 215–240.

Iwata, B., Pace, G., Kalsher, M., Cowdery, G. E., & Cataldo, M. F. (1990). Experimental analysis and extinction of self-injurious escape behavior. *Journal of Applied Behavior Analysis, 23,* 11–27.

Karen, R. L., Astin-Smith, S., & Creasy, D. (1985). Teaching telephone-answering skills to mentally retarded adults. *American Journal of Mental Deficiency, 89,* 595–609.

Kazdin, A. E., & Polster, R. (1973). Intermittent token reinforcement and response maintenance in extinction. *Behavior Therapy, 4,* 386–391.

Kennedy, C. H., Horner, R. H., Newton, J., & Kanda, E. (1990). Measuring the activity patterns of adults with severe disabilities using the Resident Lifestyle Inventory. *The Journal of the Association for Persons with Severe Handicaps, 15,* 79–85.

Koegel, R. L., & Rincover, A. (1974). Treatment of psychotic children in a classroom environment: I. Learning in a large group. *Journal of Applied Behavior Analysis, 7,* 45–59.

Koegel, R. L., & Rincover, A. (1977). Research on the difference between generalization and maintenance in extra-therapy responding. *Journal of Applied Behavior Analysis, 10,* 1–12.

Kohl, F. L., Wilcox, B. L., & Karlan, G. R. (1978). Effects of training conditions on the generalization of manual signs with moderately handicapped students. *Education and Training of the Mentally Retarded, 13,* 327–335.

Lancioni, G. E., & O'Reilly, M. F. (2001). Self-management of instruction cues for occupation: Review of studies with people with severe and profound developmental disabilities. *Research in Developmental Disabilities, 22,* 41–65.

Lancioni, G. E., O'Reilly, M. F., & Emerson, E. (1996). A review of choice research with people with severe and profound developmental disabilities. *Research in Developmental Disabilities, 17,* 391–411.

Lohrmann-O'Rourke, S., & Browder, D. M. (1998). Empirically based methods to assess the preferences of individuals with severe disabilities. *American Journal on Mental Retardation, 103,* 146–161.

Lovaas, O. I., Berberich, J. P., Perloff, B. F., & Schaeffer, B. (1966). Acquisition of imitative speech by schizophrenic children. *Science, 151,* 705–707.

Lovaas, O. I., Koegel, R. L., & Schreibman, L. (1979). Stimulus overselectivity in autism: A review of research. *Psychological Bulletin, 86,* 1236–1254.

Lovaas, O. I., Newsom, C. D., & Hickman, C. (1987). Self-stimulatory behavior and perceptual reinforcement. *Journal of Applied Behavior Analysis, 20,* 45–68.

Lovaas, O. I., & Schreibman, L. (1971). Stimulus overselectivity of autistic children in a two stimulus situation. *Behaviour Research & Therapy, 9,* 305–310.

Lovaas, O. I., Schreibman, L., Koegel, R. L., & Rehm, R. (1971). Selective responding by autistic children to multiple sensory input. *Journal of Abnormal Psychology, 77,* 211–222.

Lowry, P. W., & Ross, L. E. (1975). Severely retarded children as impulsive responders: Improved performance with response delay. *American Journal of Mental Deficiency, 80,* 133–138.

Luiselli, J. K., & Cameron, M. J. (1998). *Antecedent control: Innovative approaches to behavioral support.* Baltimore: Brookes.

Mank, D. M., & Horner, R. H. (1987). Self-recruited feedback: A cost-effective procedure for maintaining behavior. *Research in Developmental Disabilities, 8,* 91–112.

Martin, G. L., England, G. D., & England, K. G. (1971). The use of backward chaining to teach bed-making to severely retarded girls: A demonstration. *Psychological Aspects of Disability, 18,* 35–40.

Matson, J. L., Bielecki, J., Mayville, E. A., Small, Y., Bamburg, J. W., & Baglio, C. S. (1999). The development of a reinforcer choice assessment scale for persons with severe and profound mental retardation. *Research in Developmental Disabilities, 20,* 379–384.

McDonnell, J., & McFarland, S. (1988). A comparison of forward and concurrent chaining strategies in teaching laundromat skills to students with severe handicaps. *Research in Developmental Disabilities, 9,* 177–194.

McMorrow, M. J., & Foxx, R. M. (1986). Some direct and generalized effects of replacing an autistic man's echolalia with correct responses to questions. *Journal of Applied Behavior Analysis, 19,* 289–297.

McMorrow, M. J., Foxx, R. M., Faw, G. D., & Bittle, R. G. (1987). Cues–pause–point language training: Teaching echolalics functional use of their verbal labeling repertoires. *Journal of Applied Behavior Analysis, 20,* 11–22.

Meichenbaum, D., & Goodman, J. (1971). Training impulsive children to talk to themselves: A means of developing self-control. *Journal of Abnormal Psychology, 77,* 115–126.

Mithaug, D. E., & Hanawalt, D. A. (1978). The validation of procedures to assess prevocational task preferences in retarded adults. *Journal of Applied Behavior Analysis, 11*, 153–162.

Mithaug, D. E., & Mar, D. K. (1980). The relation between choosing and working on prevocational tasks in two severely retarded young adults. *Journal of Applied Behavior Analysis, 13*, 177–182.

O'Reilly, M. F. (1995). Functional analysis and treatment of escape-maintained aggression correlated with sleep deprivation. *Journal of Applied Behavior Analysis, 28*, 225–226.

O'Reilly, M. F. (1997). Functional analysis of episodic self-injury correlated with recurrent otitis media. *Journal of Applied Behavior Analysis, 30*, 165–167.

O'Reilly, M. F., Lacey, C., & Lancioni, G. E. (2000). Assessment of the influence of background noise on escape-maintained problem behavior and pain behavior in a child with Williams syndrome. *Journal of Applied Behavior Analysis, 33*, 511–514.

Ortiz, K., & Carr, J. (2000). Multiple-stimulus preference assessments: A comparison of free-operant and restricted-operant formats. *Behavioral Interventions, 15*, 345–353.

Pace, G. M., Ivancic, M. T., Edwards, G. L., Iwata, B. A., & Page, T. J. (1985). Assessment of stimulus preference and reinforcer value with profoundly retarded individuals. *Journal of Applied Behavior Analysis, 18*, 249–255.

Pace, G. M., Iwata, B. A., Cowdery, G., Andree, P., & McIntyre, T. (1993). Stimulus (instructional) fading during extinction of self-injurious escape behavior. *Journal of Applied Behavior Analysis, 26*, 205–212.

Paclawskyj, T., & Vollmer, T. R. (1995). Reinforcer assessment for children with developmental disabilities and visual impairments. *Journal of Applied Behavior Analysis, 28*, 219–224.

Parmenter, T. R. (1994). Quality of life as a concept and measurable entity. *Social Indicators Research, 33*, 9–46.

Piazza, C. C., Fisher, W. W., Hagopian, L. H., Bowman, L. B., & Toole, L. (1996). Using a choice assessment to predict reinforcer effectiveness. *Journal of Applied Behavior Analysis, 29*, 1–9.

Riley, G. A. (1993). *The use of prompts in teaching people with a learning disability.* Unpublished doctoral dissertation, University of Leicester, UK.

Riley, G. A. (1995). Guidelines for devising a hierarchy when fading response prompts. *Education and Training in Mental Retardation and Developmental Disabilities, 30*, 231–242.

Roberts-Pennell, D., & Sigafoos, J. (1999). Teaching young children with developmental disabilities to request more play using the behavior chain interruption strategy. *Journal of Applied Research in Intellectual Disability, 12*, 100–112.

Schleien, S. J., Wehman, P., & Kiernan, J. (1981). Teaching leisure skills to severely handicapped adults: An age-appropriate darts game. *Journal of Applied Behavior Analysis, 14,* 513–519.

Schoen, S. F. (1986). Assistance procedures to facilitate the transfer of stimulus control: Review and analysis. *Education and Training of the Mentally Retarded, 21,* 62–74.

Schreibman, L. (1975). Effects of within-stimulus and extra-stimulus prompting on discrimination learning in autistic children. *Journal of Applied Behavior Analysis, 8,* 91–112.

Sigafoos, J. (1992). Augmenting unintelligible speech with a graphic communication system. *Mental Handicap in New Zealand, 12*(4), 3–8.

Sigafoos, J. (1998). Choice making and personal selection strategies. In J. K. Luiselli & M. J. Cameron (Eds.), *Antecedent control: Innovative approaches to behavioral support* (pp. 187–221). Baltimore: Brookes.

Sigafoos, J., & Dempsey, R. (1992). Assessing choice-making among children with multiple disabilities. *Journal of Applied Behavior Analysis, 25,* 747–755.

Sigafoos, J., & DePaepe, P. (1994). Writing IPP objectives to replace challenging behaviors with functional, age-appropriate alternatives. *Journal of Practical Approaches to Developmental Handicaps, 18*(2), 24–28.

Sigafoos, J., Didden, R., & O'Reilly, M. (2003). Effects of speech output on maintenance of requesting and frequency of vocalizations in three children with developmental disabilities. *Augmentative and Alternative Communication, 19,* 37–47.

Sigafoos, J., Doss, S., & Reichle, J. (1989). Developing mand and tact repertoires in persons with developmental disabilities using graphic symbols. *Research in Developmental Disabilities, 10,* 183–200.

Sigafoos, J., Laurie, S., & Pennell, D. (1995). Preliminary assessment of choice making among children with Rett syndrome. *Journal of the Association for Persons with Severe Handicaps, 20,* 175–184.

Skinner, B. F. (1953). *Science and human behavior.* New York: Macmillan.

Skinner, B. F. (1968). *The technology of teaching.* New York: Meredith.

Smeets, P. M., & Kleinloog, D. (1980). Teaching retarded women to use an experimental pocket calculator for making financial transactions. *Behavior Research of Severely Developmentally Disabled, 1,* 1–20.

Smeets, P. M., & Striefel, S. (1976a). Acquisition of sign reading by transfer of stimulus control in a retarded deaf girl. *Journal of Mental Deficiency Research, 20,* 197–205.

Smeets, P. M., & Striefel, S. (1976b). Acquisition and cross modal generalization of receptive and expressive signing skills in a retarded deaf girl. *Journal of Mental Deficiency Research, 20,* 251–260.

Smith, R. G., Iwata, B. A., Goh, H., & Shore, B. A. (1995). Analysis of establishing operations for self-injury maintained by escape. *Journal of Applied Behavior Analysis, 28,* 515–535.

Snell, M. E., & Kneedler, R. (1978). *Acquisition of waiting behavior as a prerequisite to delayed instruction.* Unpublished manuscript.

Stancliffe, R. J. (1995). Assessing opportunities for choice-making: A comparison of self and staff reports. *American Journal on Mental Retardation, 99,* 418–429.

Steele, D. A. (1977). *Transfer of stimulus control via temporal fading: Experimental analysis.* Unpublished doctoral dissertation, Utah State University, Logan.

Stokes, T. F., Baer, D. M., & Jackson, R. L. (1974). Programming the generalization of a greeting response in four retarded children. *Journal of Applied Behavior Analysis, 7,* 599–610.

Stokes, T. F., & Osnes, P. G. (1989). An operant pursuit of generalization. *Behavior Therapy, 20,* 337–355.

Stremel-Campbell, K., Cantrell, D., & Halle, J. W. (1977). Manual signing as a language system and as a speech initiator for the nonverbal severely handicapped student. In E. Sontag, J. Smith, & N. Certo (Eds.), *Educational programming for the severely and profoundly handicapped* (pp. 335–347). Reston, VA: Division on Mental Retardation, Council for Exceptional Children.

Striefel, S., Bryan, K. S., & Aikins, D. A. (1974). Transfer of stimulus control from motor to verbal stimuli. *Journal of Applied Behavior Analysis, 7,* 123–135.

Sturmey, P. (1995). Analog baselines: A critical review of the methodology. *Research in Developmental Disabilities, 16,* 269–284.

Taylor, J., Ekdahl, M., Romanczyk, R., & Miller, M. (1994). Escape behavior in task situations: Task versus social antecedents. *Journal of Autism and Developmental Disorders, 24,* 331–344.

Touchette, P. E. (1971). Transfer of stimulus control: Measuring the moment of transfer. *Journal of the Experimental Analysis of Behavior, 15,* 347–354.

Touchette, P. E., & Howard, J. S. (1984). Errorless learning: Reinforcement contingencies and stimulus control transfer in delayed prompting. *Journal of Applied Behavior Analysis, 17,* 175–188.

Vaughn, B., & Horner, R. H. (1995). Effects of concrete versus verbal choice systems on problem behavior. *Augmentative and Alternative Communication, 11,* 89–92.

Vollmer, T. R., Marcus, B. A., & Ringdahl, J. E. (1995). Noncontingent escape as treatment for self-injurious behavior maintained by negative reinforcement. *Journal of Applied Behavior Analysis, 28,* 15–26.

Walls, R. T., Ellis, W. D., Zane, T., & Vanderpoel, S. J. (1979). Tactile, auditory, and visual prompting in teaching complex assembly tasks. *Education and Training of the Mentally Retarded, 14,* 120–130.

Watters, R. G., Wheeler, L. J., & Watters, W. E. (1981). The relative efficiency of two orders for training autistic children in the expressive and receptive use of manual signs. *Journal of Communication Disorders, 14,* 273–285.

Weeks, M., & Gaylord-Ross, R. (1981). Task difficulty and aberrant behavior in severely handicapped students. *Journal of Applied Behavior Analysis, 14*, 449–463.

Wilcox, B., & Bellamy, T. (1982). *Design of high school programs for severely handicapped students.* Baltimore: Brookes.

Windsor, J., Piché, L. M., & Locke, P. A. (1994). Preference testing: A comparison of two presentation methods. *Research in Developmental Disabilities, 15*, 439–455.

Wolery, M., & Gast, D. L. (1984). Effective and efficient procedures for the transfer of stimulus control. *Topics in Early Childhood Special Education, 4*, 52–77.

Wright, C. W., & Schuster, J. W. (1994). Accepting specific versus functional student responses when training chained tasks. *Education and Training in Mental Retardation and Developmental Disabilities, 29*, 43–56.

Index

◆◆◆◆◆◆◆◆◆◆◆◆◆◆◆◆◆◆◆◆◆◆◆◆◆◆

About the Authors

◆◆◆◆◆◆◆◆◆◆◆◆◆◆◆◆◆◆◆◆◆◆◆◆◆◆◆◆◆◆◆◆

Pieter C. Duker, PhD, is a professor in developmental disabilities at the University of Nijmegen, and a psychologist at the Pluryn Foundation, a residential facility for individuals with developmental disabilities in Nijmegen, The Netherlands. His clinical and research interests include developing new and more effective procedures for teaching communicative skills, especially the use of gesture communication for children who do not have speech. He has also developed innovative procedures for establishing toileting skills in learners with developmental disabilities. His current research focuses on the assessment and treatment of self-injurious behavior in individuals with autism and related developmental disabilities, including treatments to address extreme forms of life-threatening self-injurious behaviors. Duker has published approximately 70 articles in international journals. He serves on the editorial boards of the *Journal of Intellectual Disability Research* and *Research in Developmental Disabilities.*

Robert Didden, PhD, is an assistant professor in developmental disabilities at the University of Nijmegen, The Netherlands. He participates in training undergraduate and graduate students and maintains an active research program on teaching individuals with developmental disabilities. He has authored several articles and books on the education and treatment of individuals with developmental disabilities. In addition to his position at the University of Nijmegen, he is a psychologist at the Zozijn Foundation, a facility for individuals with developmental disabilities in The Netherlands. As a consultant, he is also involved in the functional analysis and treatment of severe problem behaviors in children and adults with developmental disabilities. Didden is an associate editor for *Perceptual and Motor Skills* and for the Dutch-language journal *Nederlands Tijdschrift voor de Zorg aan Verstandelijk Gehandicapten.*

Jeff Sigafoos, PhD, is a professor in the Department of Special Education at The University of Texas at Austin. Prior to this, he was a professor in special education at The University of Sydney and held a joint appointment with the Children's Hospital in Sydney, Australia. Sigafoos has authored or co-authored over 100 articles on educating individuals with developmental disabilities and has been awarded 26 research grants to develop effective interventions for communication training and for the treatment of severe behavior problems in children with autism and related developmental and physical disabilities. He is past editor of the *International Journal of Disability, Development and Education* and associate editor of *Augmentative and Alternative Communication.* He also serves on the editorial boards of 11 journals. In 1995, he received the National Research Prize from the Australian Society for the Study of Intellectual Disability for his research on the assessment of severe behavior problems.